THE EVERYTHING KIDS'®

DUMP TRUCKS & BULLDOZERS

PUZZLE AND ACTIVITY BOOK

THE EVERYTHING KIDS' DUMP TRUCKS & BULLDOZERS PUZZLE AND ACTIVITY BOOK

Load, lift, dig, and dump with
100 down-and-dirty puzzles

Beth L. Blair and Jennifer A. Ericsson

adamsmedia
Avon, Massachusetts

PUBLISHER Karen Cooper

MANAGING EDITOR, EVERYTHING® SERIES Lisa Laing

COPY CHIEF Casey Ebert

ASSISTANT PRODUCTION EDITOR Jo-Anne Duhamel

ACQUISITIONS EDITOR Lisa Laing

DEVELOPMENT EDITOR Lisa Laing

EVERYTHING® SERIES COVER DESIGNER Erin Alexander

An Everything® Series Book.
Everything® and everything.com® are registered trademarks of F+W Media, Inc.

Published by Adams Media, a division of F+W Media, Inc.
57 Littlefield Street, Avon, MA 02322. U.S.A.
www.adamsmedia.com

ISBN 10: 1-5072-0119-2
ISBN 13: 978-1-5072-0119-0

Printed by RR Donnelley, Harrisonburg, VA, U.S.A.

10 9 8 7 6 5 4 3 2 1

September 2016

Many of the designations used by manufacturers and sellers to distinguish their
products are claimed as trademarks. Where those designations appear in this book
and F+W Media, Inc. was aware of a trademark claim, the designations have been
printed with initial capital letters.

Cover illustrations by Dana Regan.
Interior illustrations by Kurt Dolber.
Puzzles by Beth L. Blair.

This book is available at quantity discounts for bulk purchases.
For information, please call 1-800-289-0963.

Visit the entire Everything® series at www.everything.com

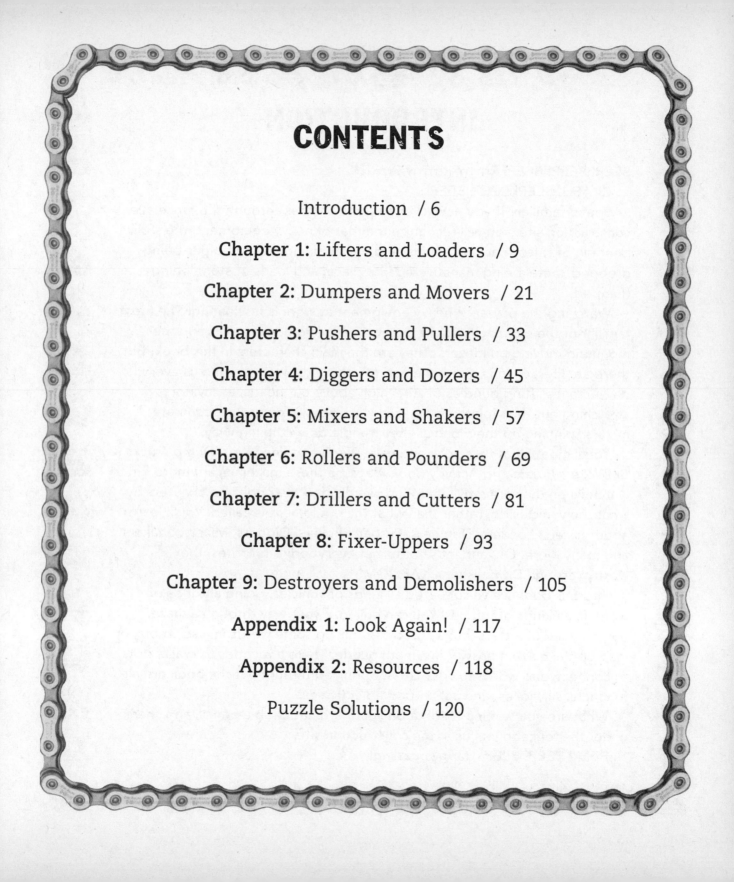

CONTENTS

Introduction / 6

Chapter 1: Lifters and Loaders / 9

Chapter 2: Dumpers and Movers / 21

Chapter 3: Pushers and Pullers / 33

Chapter 4: Diggers and Dozers / 45

Chapter 5: Mixers and Shakers / 57

Chapter 6: Rollers and Pounders / 69

Chapter 7: Drillers and Cutters / 81

Chapter 8: Fixer-Uppers / 93

Chapter 9: Destroyers and Demolishers / 105

Appendix 1: Look Again! / 117

Appendix 2: Resources / 118

Puzzle Solutions / 120

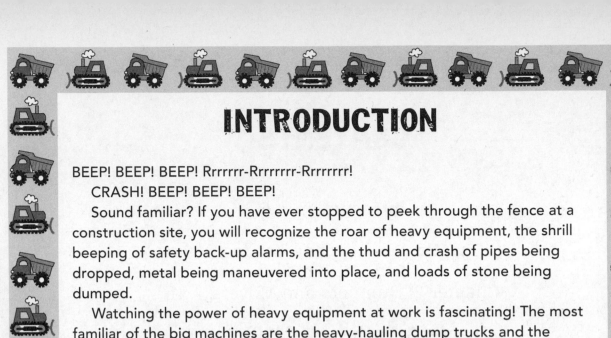

INTRODUCTION

BEEP! BEEP! BEEP! Rrrrrrr-Rrrrrrrr-Rrrrrrrr!

CRASH! BEEP! BEEP! BEEP!

Sound familiar? If you have ever stopped to peek through the fence at a construction site, you will recognize the roar of heavy equipment, the shrill beeping of safety back-up alarms, and the thud and crash of pipes being dropped, metal being maneuvered into place, and loads of stone being dumped.

Watching the power of heavy equipment at work is fascinating! The most familiar of the big machines are the heavy-hauling dump trucks and the mountain-moving bulldozers. They are the main characters in this book. But there are literally tons of other amazing vehicles at work around us every day—cranes lifting bundles of steel high above our heads, excavators stretching out their jointed arms like weird metallic dinosaurs, concrete mixers spinning up their load as they trundle down the highway.

You'll meet all of these characters in *The Everything® Kids' Dump Trucks & Bulldozers Puzzle and Activity Book*. Because these machines are more fun to watch when they are moving around, we divided the book into chapters by what the vehicles do, rather than what the equipment is called. You'll learn about Lifters, Loaders, Dumpers, Pushers, Pullers, Diggers, Mixers, Shakers, and many more. Oh, and let's not forget everybody's favorites, the Destroyers and Demolishers. KABOOM!

Into this book we've squeezed all kinds of vehicles, doing all kinds of work, in all kinds of puzzles! You can bulldoze your way through a maze, dump a load of letters into a crisscross, mix up some words in a scramble, or load up the correct answer in a math puzzle. There are codes to crack, dots to connect, and words to criss-cross. Sprinkled throughout the book are also fun facts, silly jokes, and action-packed activities.

What are you waiting for? Put on your hard hat, grab a pencil, and sneak under the fence to join us at the construction site.

BEEP! BEEP! BEEP! Happy puzzling!

GET READY FOR FUN!

Sift through this letter grid to find twelve construction vehicles. Words can be found in any direction, including backwards and diagonally!

Word List

- SKIDDER
- GRADER
- LOADER
- TRACTOR
- DUMP TRUCK
- CRANE
- EXCAVATOR
- BULLDOZER
- BACKHOE
- MIXER
- ROLLER
- FORKLIFT

```
T F I L K R O F R T S T M O
B A S T O U S N R E O P I N
U B A C K H O E G I D B X E
L U P O R T D N A C R A E T
L A R T R A C T O R A Z R U
D C E Q O Y P E R S C O N G
O K L L E D U M P T R U C K
Z L L N R U N N T O A O M S
E M O S K I D D E R N S T M
R Z R O T A V A C X E I E F
```

CHAPTER 1
LIFTERS AND LOADERS

FOUR AND MORE

This forklift can move only four boxes at a time. How many trips will it take to load all the boxes onto a trailer?

EXTRA FUN: Find the four boxes that have the exact same label. Then find the one box that has a unique label!

10

TIGHT SPACES

A skid steer loader is a small construction vehicle that can turn around in very tight spaces. It does this by slowing down or stopping the wheels on one side while the wheels on the other side continue to turn. Help this driver maneuver out from the center of this construction site. At which corner will he end up?

FLOATING CRANES

Structures surrounded by water, such as offshore drilling platforms and bridges, are built using huge cranes that are floated out to the work site. Solve this puzzle to find the name for the gigantic, flat boat that carries the crane!

Each clue suggests a word. Write the words you come up with in the shaded circles. When you are finished, write the letters in the darker circles on the dotted lines. HINT: The last letter of one word is the first letter of the next!

1. **Long, yellow fruit**
2. **What a knight wears**
3. **Another name for carpet**
4. **Liquid adhesive**

1.

2.

3.

4.

The flat boat that carries a crane is a __ __ __ __ __.

UP AND DOWN

Bulldozers and dump trucks are constantly moving things up and down! Connect the dots horizontally and vertically to divide these words into two groups. On one side should be all the words that have a meaning similar to UP. On the other side should be all the words that have a meaning similar to DOWN.

reach   lift   fall

over   stoop   below

climb   under   beneath

soar   ascend   drop

hoist   elevate   lower

boost   descend   bottom

raise   cut   crashed

higher   low   sink

aloft   above   overhead

GOING UP

This telescopic crane has an extendable arm that reaches up as far as it needs to go. The word CRANE is written next to the base of the arm. Delete one letter at a time to form a new word on the next line. Keep deleting letters until you have a one-letter word at the very top of the crane!

CRANE

13

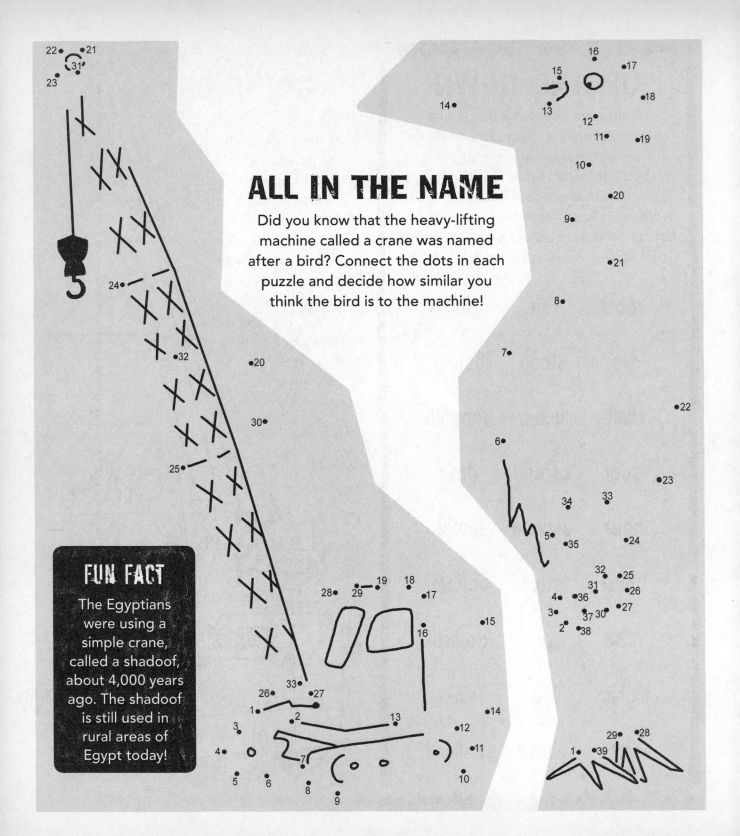

ALL IN THE NAME

Did you know that the heavy-lifting machine called a crane was named after a bird? Connect the dots in each puzzle and decide how similar you think the bird is to the machine!

FUN FACT

The Egyptians were using a simple crane, called a shadoof, about 4,000 years ago. The shadoof is still used in rural areas of Egypt today!

14

JUNK PILE

To solve this puzzle, name the pictures at the top of the junk pile. Follow the line from each picture to a box at the bottom. Write the first letter of the picture into the box!

A ▢▢▢▢▢▢▢ is

a grabbing tool used by cranes to pick up heavy things.

15

JUST JOKING

Start at the white letter. Follow the arrows to get you started, and zig-zag up the scissor-like legs of the lift, reading all the letters on the left. Then, zig-zag your way back down, reading the letters on the right. When you are finished, you will know the answer to this riddle!

Three large men were huddled at the top of an aerial lift. They were squished under one small umbrella. How many men got wet?

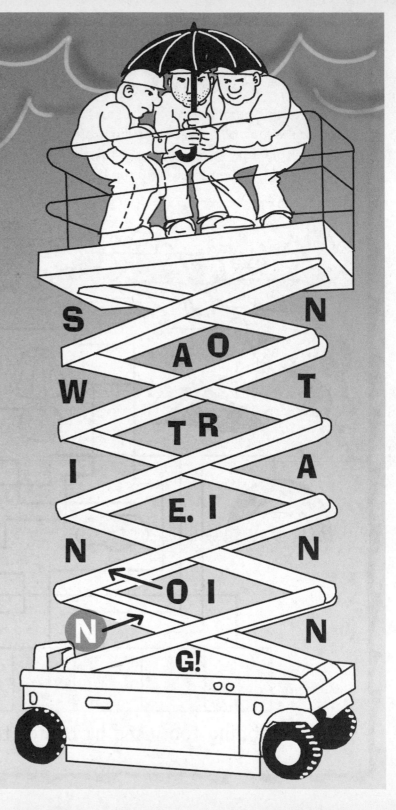

EGG DROP

Drop each letter into one of the spaces directly underneath it. All the letters will remain in the same column. When you have the letters in their correct places, you will know the answer to this riddle.

How can a crane drop an egg 50 feet without breaking it?

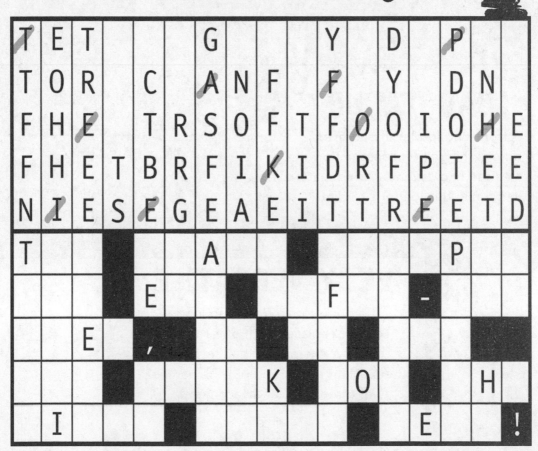

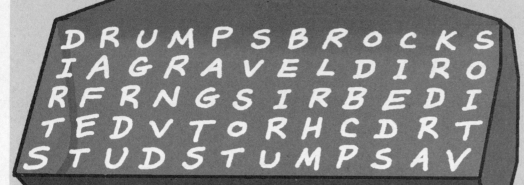

```
D R U M P S B R O C K S
I A G R A V E L D I R O
R F R N G S I R B E D I
T E D V T O R H C D R T
S T U D S T U M P S A V
```

SOIL
ROCKS
GRAVEL
DEBRIS
DIRT
SAND
STUMPS

LOAD 'EM UP

A front-end loader lifts, moves, and dumps things at a construction site. See if you can find seven building materials hidden in this loader's bucket.

VERY VERSATILE

The bucket on a front-end loader can be replaced with other tools. Solve the picture and letter equations and sound out the names of three popular attachments!

1. **R +** 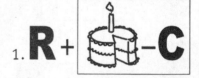 **– C**

2.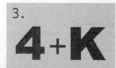

3. **4 + K**

18

WAY TO MOVE

There are two different ways that loaders move from one place to another. Use the decoder to learn what these are.

A ⊙
C ⊗
E ○
H ✹
K ⚙
L 🗝
R 〰
S 〰
T ///
W ⌃⌃

Some front loaders get around by using

⌃⌃ ✹ ○ ○ 🗝 〰 .

Other front loaders use

/// 〰 ⊙ ⊗ ⚙ 〰 .

Which way is more popular? Complete the letter equations, and read the answer from right to left to find out!

$$(Q+2)(N-2)(F-I)(A+4)(C+5)(Z-3)$$

WINDOW DELIVERY

A special kind of crane hoists supplies to places that are hard to reach. It has a joint that keeps the load level when passing through a window. To learn this loader's silly name, solve the word fractions and write the answers in the windows of the building from left to right, and top to bottom. Read the answer the same way!

1. First $\frac{1}{3}$ of **KEY**
2. First $\frac{2}{3}$ of **NUT**
3. Last $\frac{2}{5}$ of **TRUCK**
4. Middle $\frac{2}{3}$ of **OILERS**
5. First $\frac{1}{2}$ of **BOSS**
6. Second $\frac{1}{4}$ of **LOAD**
7. Last $\frac{1}{4}$ of **BEAM**

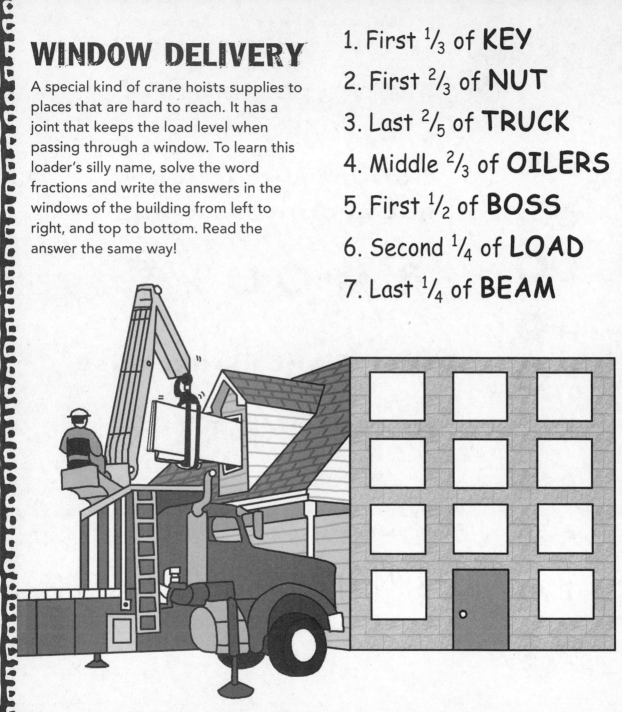

CHAPTER 2
DUMPERS AND MOVERS

DIFFERENT DUMPERS

Dump trucks come in many sizes and dump their loads
in different ways. Some dump out the back, some
from underneath, and some even dump sideways! Fit
the nine different dump trucks into the crisscross.
We've left some D-I-R-T to get you started!

STANDARD

SEMI-TRAILER

ARTICULATED

TRANSFER

SUPERDUMP

BELLY DUMP

END DUMP   SIDE DUMP   TRUCK AND PUP

NOISY NAME

The transfer dump truck makes a particularly loud noise when transferring a load. Fill in the shapes that have the letters L-O-U-D to learn this dump truck's funny nickname!

FILL 'ER UP

To find the silly answer to the riddle, add up all the numbers carried by these dump trucks. Write the total in the shaded box. Then transfer the three letters from the door of each truck, in order, onto the dotted lines.

How many rocks can you put in an empty dump truck?

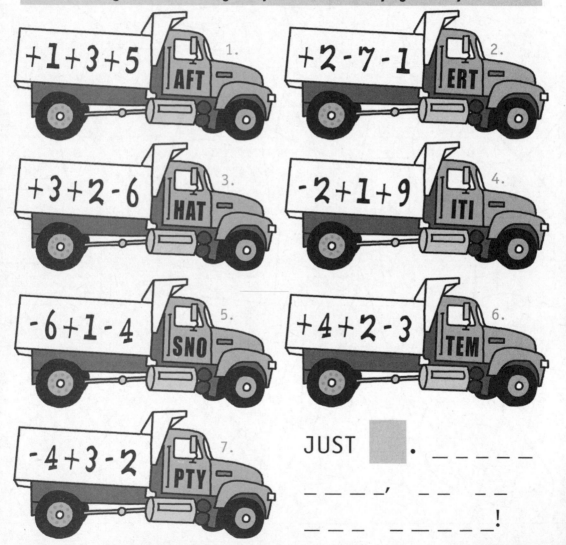

1. $+1+3+5$ — AFT
2. $+2-7-1$ — ERT
3. $+3+2-6$ — HAT
4. $-2+1+9$ — ITI
5. $-6+1-4$ — SNO
6. $+4+2-3$ — TEM
7. $-4+3-2$ — PTY

JUST ____ . _ _ _ _ _ _

_ _ _ _ _ , _ _ _ _

_ _ _ _ _ _ !

24

TONS OF TRASH

This garbage truck has just dumped a load of trash at the landfill. It is amazing what people will throw out!

Can you figure out the 16 items that begin with the letter "T"?

SAFE TRAVELS

A full dump truck must have its load covered to keep loose materials from flying out and causing damage. Sift through the D-I-R-T in this truck bed to find five items used to do the job.

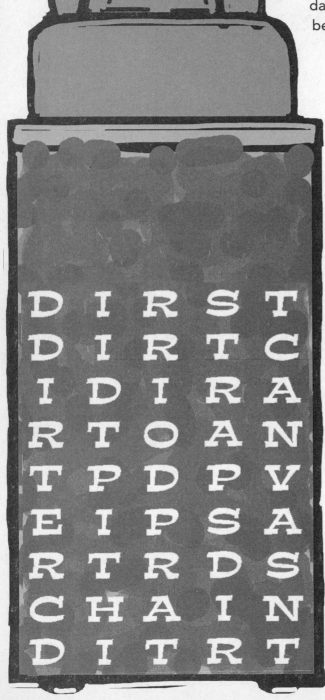

CUBIC WHAT?

The materials loaded into a dump truck are measured in cubic yards. But what are those? Match the patterns, and color in the correct cubes to get the answer.

A cubic yard is

color this pattern /

feet high

color this pattern >

feet long

color this pattern v

feet wide

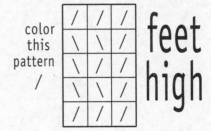

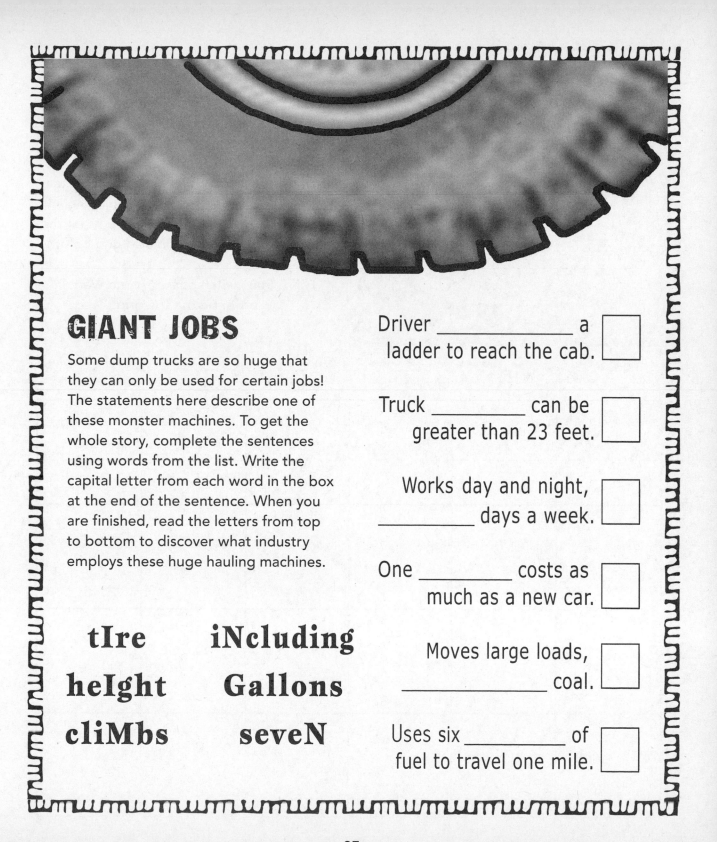

GIANT JOBS

Some dump trucks are so huge that they can only be used for certain jobs! The statements here describe one of these monster machines. To get the whole story, complete the sentences using words from the list. Write the capital letter from each word in the box at the end of the sentence. When you are finished, read the letters from top to bottom to discover what industry employs these huge hauling machines.

tIre

heIght

cliMbs

iNcluding

Gallons

seveN

Driver _____ a ladder to reach the cab. ☐

Truck _____ can be greater than 23 feet. ☐

Works day and night, _____ days a week. ☐

One _____ costs as much as a new car. ☐

Moves large loads, _____ coal. ☐

Uses six _____ of fuel to travel one mile. ☐

FAST FUNNY

Break the code (1=A, 2=B, etc.) to learn the riddle's silly answer. Hint: Try reading each letter of the answer out loud!

What did the driver say to his truck after he dumped out the load of rock?

15-9-3-21

18-13-20!

DUH!

SO BIG!

A giant dump truck, such as the kind used in mining operations, is much too big to travel on an ordinary road. Before it moves to a new job site, it has to be taken apart. Then it is carried on a special transporter to its new location. You can rebuild a giant dump truck by copying the patterns on the next page into the numbered grid below.

HINT: Start with square 1A and work in order across the grid.

	A	B	C	D	E	F
1						
2						
3						
4						

GREEN TIRES?

Making heavy-duty tires for dump trucks, trailers, and loaders is no simple task! Each tire has six parts: treads, body ply, belts, sidewalls, inner liner, and beads. Once all the raw components are assembled, the soft and gummy (or "green") tire is put in a special mold. Huge amounts of pressure and heat are used to transform the soft rubber into a strong and durable tire. What is one high-tech way that manufacturers check that each new tire is safe and free of defects? Connect the dots to find out!

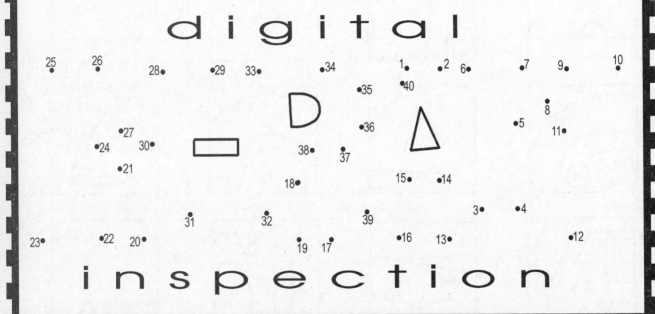

d i g i t a l

25 26   28 29 33   34   1 2 6   7 9   10
                            40
              35   8
        27   D   36   5   11
    24   30
    21   38
                    37
              18   15 14
        31   32   39   3 4
23   22 20   16 13   12
        19 17

i n s p e c t i o n

FUNNY FLATS

Moving from place to place takes its toll on construction vehicles—especially their tires. Break the Vowel Switch code to get the silly answer to this riddle!

Q: When do dump trucks get the most flat tires?

A: Whun thuru as o ferk an thu reod!

TWISTED SKIDDERS

Skidders are forestry machines that pull felled logs through the woods. A blade on the front pushes debris out of the way. This can get very messy! The skidders on this page are not moving logs, they are pulling shapes. Everything has gotten all twisted up! Can you figure out which skidder is pulling the most shapes? Which shape appears only once?

FAST FORWARD

A forwarder is a vehicle that carries logs from where they were cut in the forest to where they are loaded onto a truck for transport. It carries them in the bed of the truck (off the ground), unlike the skidder which pulls them across the ground. Once the forwarder reaches the main road, a bendable arm and grapple are used to unload the logs. Grab some friends and pretend to be forwarders. It's not an easy job!

What You Need

round toothpicks
    (at least 1 box = 250)
tweezers
    (1 pair for each player)
bowls (1 for each player)
timer

What You Do

- Dump the round toothpicks on a flat surface like a table or floor. These are your felled logs.

- Each player is assigned a bowl. All bowls are placed the same distance away on the other side of the room.

- Set the timer for two minutes. Each player tries to pick up and carry as many logs as possible to their bowl using only the tweezers. Players make as many trips back and forth as they can in the two-minute time period. If a player drops any of their logs on the way to their bowl, they must stop and retrieve them.

- The player with the most logs in their bowl at the end of two minutes wins!

Game Variations

- Slow or Fast: Add or subtract the number of minutes on the timer depending on the number of players and the number of logs available. If you only have one pair of tweezers, take turns and race the clock. See who has the most logs in their bowl after everyone has had a turn.

- Eat the Logs: Use skinny pretzel sticks as an alternative to toothpicks. However, if you plan to eat the logs afterwards, do not dump them on the floor — ick!

- Bigger Fun: Toothpicks and pretzel sticks too small for you? Try using pretzel logs and kitchen tongs instead!

SPLASH!

Each numbered clue suggests a word. Write each answer on the dotted lines, then read the circled letters from top to bottom.

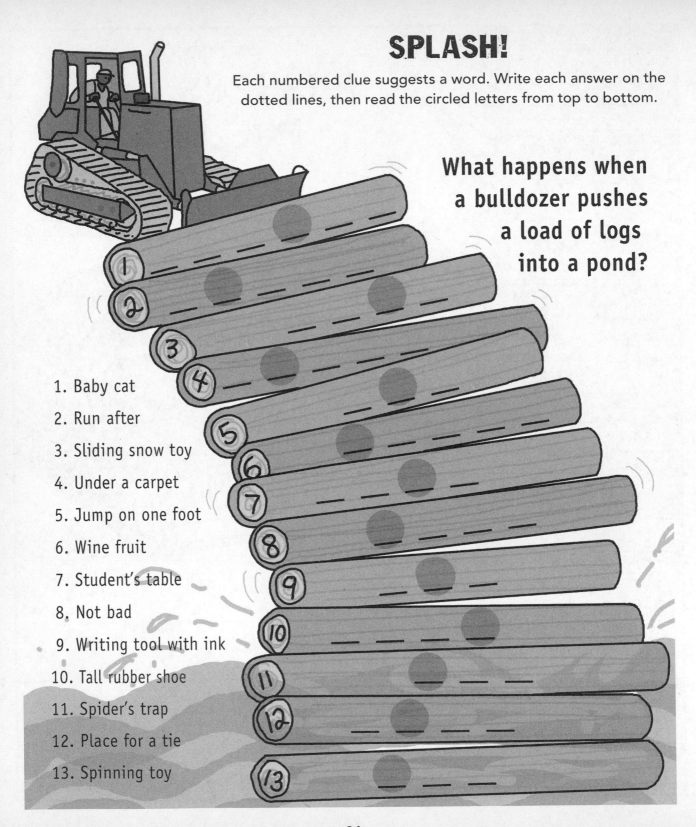

What happens when a bulldozer pushes a load of logs into a pond?

1. Baby cat

2. Run after

3. Sliding snow toy

4. Under a carpet

5. Jump on one foot

6. Wine fruit

7. Student's table

8. Not bad

9. Writing tool with ink

10. Tall rubber shoe

11. Spider's trap

12. Place for a tie

13. Spinning toy

DRAG, DRAW,
HAUL, JERK,
MOVE, NUDGE,
PROPEL, PULL,
PUSH, SHOVE,
THRUST, TOW,
TUG, YANK

PUSH ME, PULL YOU

Some machines pull loads, and others push them. Either way, things get moved! Can you find the 14 push or pull action words hidden in the grid?

```
N O D T Y A S P U S H K
W I R R O H S R T P U K
T S A U T W M O V E P N
I M G P A R Y P T H S A
E U R N U D G E O S H Y
T F O A L L R L T H T U
H A U L G I L K W O M N
R M P O O U Y A J V O U
U E N T P E A I D E V D
S O C O T O T H O F R R
T T H M E D R A W G T K
```

VERY VISIBLE

Take a dark marker or crayon and color in the letters facing the WRONG way. The remaining letters will spell out the color that is most often used to paint heavy equipment. This color is easily seen on a construction site! Use a marker or crayon of that color to fill in the answer letters.

KYRYEE
BSTEB
TESDY
KGBOZ
JLWES

BIG AND SMALL

Some snowplows are huge, and some are teensy. Use the decoder to figure out what jobs different-sized plows can do!

❋=A ❋=E ❋=I ✳=O ❋=U ✳=Y

GIANT SNOWPLOWS CLEAR
❋❋RP✳RT R✳NW❋✳S

TINY SNOWPLOWS CLEAR
C✳T✳ S❋D❋W❋LKS

STORM CLEANUP

After a big blizzard, plows need to push the snow out of the streets. Which of these sets of turns will steer a snowplow around the entire neighborhood? (R=Right, L=Left)

1. R, L, L, R, R, L
2. R, R, L, R, L, R
3. R, 2nd L, L, R, L, L
4. R, 2nd L, L, L, L, R

enter

exit

WHAT'S THE DIFFERENCE?

These two grader operators may look pretty much alike, but can you find the eight differences?

DYNAMIC DUO

Graders and scrapers are heavy-duty vehicles used to level lumpy and pitted dirt roads, building sites, and parking areas. Even though they do the same kind of job, they are not the same machine! Cross off each word that is in both the top field AND the bottom field. Read the remaining words, in order, from left to right and top to bottom to discover the main difference between these two pieces of equipment.

THE ONLY MACHINE THAT ROCKS
BIG SCRAPER LIFTS UP BLADE
CARRIES GROUND IS BLACK DIRT
RIGHT ANGLE TO DRAG ALONG

LIFTS FILL UP GROUND IN
DRAG BLADE ONLY ALL MACHINE
IS ALONG LOW ROCKS ANGLE
BIG AREAS RIGHT BLACK THAT

WORLD WIDE

What company is the largest maker of heavy equipment in the world? Break the code at the bottom of the page to reveal its name!

EXTRA FUN: What three letters are clearly visible on each piece of their equipment? Use a black crayon or marker to fill in all the shapes with a + in the middle. Now color the rest of the machine bright yellow!

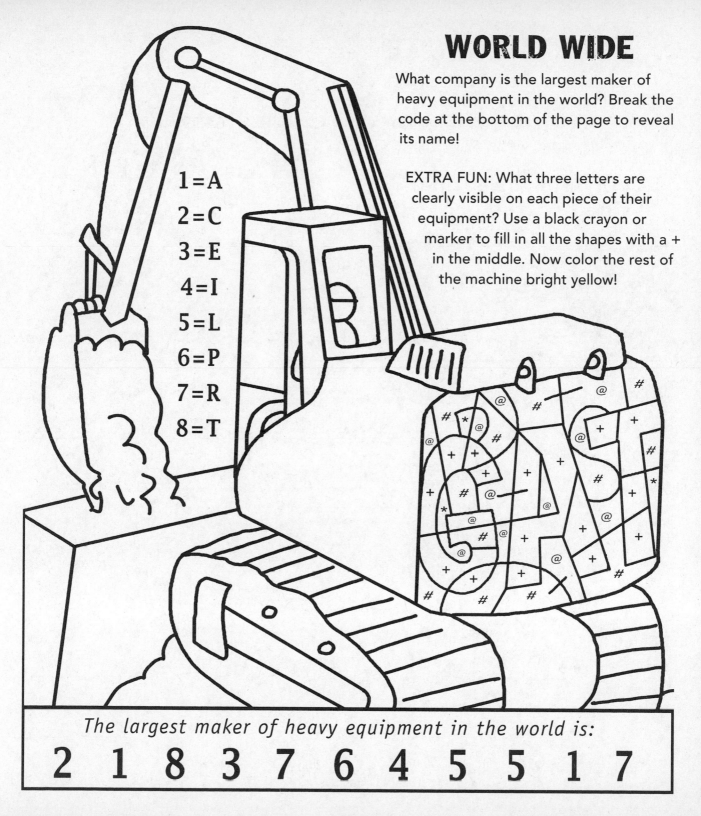

1 = A
2 = C
3 = E
4 = I
5 = L
6 = P
7 = R
8 = T

The largest maker of heavy equipment in the world is:

2   1   8   3   7   6   4   5   5   1   7

FUNNY FARMER

Take a trip with this farmer through his field from START to END, picking up letters as you go. When you are finished, read the letters you have collected to find the silly answer to this serious question!

Why did the farmer ride his tractor?

START

END

TRACTOR TREADS

The treads on a tractor's tires are very deep—and for a good reason!
Crack the Reverse Alphabet code (Z=A, Y=B, X=C, etc.) to find out their function.

GSv   WVVK   GIVZwH   NZPv

RG   ZONLHG   RNKLHHRYOV

ULI   GSv   GIZXGLI   GL   TVG

YLTTVW   wLDM   RM   GSv   NFw

BACKWARDS BACKFILL

Bulldozers, graders, and other pushing vehicles do not just push forward. They can also pull back with their blade. When dirt is moved in this way, it is called "backfilling." Find the correct path from the "backyard" to the "roadside" as you travel backwards from the bottom right-hand corner of the puzzle. Create compound words by moving one space up, down, or side-to-side. Do not move diagonally!

END

SIDE	ROAD	RIGHT	UP
CAR	RAIL	HAND	STICK
SEAT	WAY	STEP	YARD
BELT	DOWN	SIDE	BACK

START

HORSE POWER

When engines were first replacing horses to do heavy work, people wanted a way to compare their strength. The term "horsepower" was invented, but what does it mean? To find out, locate all the threes in this horse. Add them up and write the total in the shaded box. Then break the Vowel Switch code, and use a dark marker to write in the correct vowels.

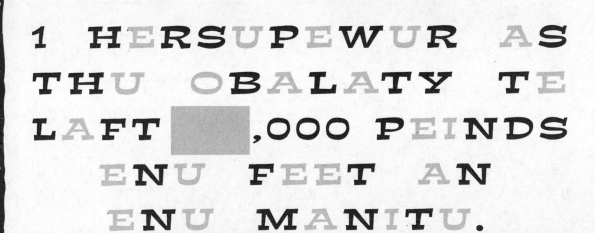

1 HERSUPEWUR AS THU OBALATY TE LAFT ▊,000 PEINDS ENU FEET AN ENU MANITU.

CUT UP

Large tractors are generally used for farming, but many construction sites use smaller versions for landscaping jobs. These tiny tractors are called CUTs. Piece together the cut-up words onto the blank puzzle grid. When you are done, read from left to right to find the full name of these compact machines.

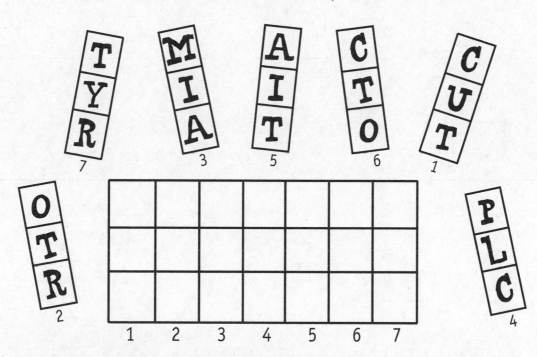

TINY PUZZLE

What one letter can you add to CUT to describe these mini machines? Fill in the blank to complete the tractor's caption!

Awww, aren't you CUT__!

43

WACKY TRACKS

Four different dozers have been working at the same construction site. Looking at the tracks left in the dirt, which piece of equipment made the most trips across the site?

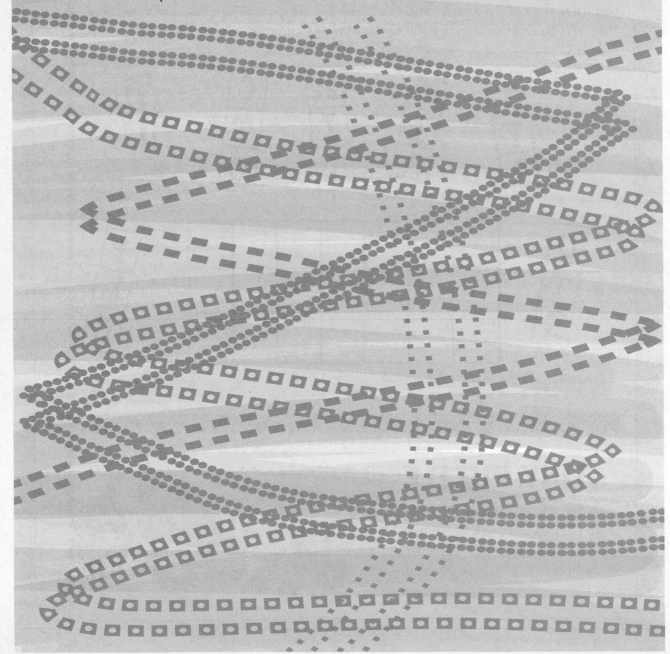

CHAPTER 4
DIGGERS AND DOZERS

AMAZING INVENTOR

In his lifetime (1888–1969), Robert G. LeTourneau held nearly 300 patents that improved scrapers, bulldozers, cranes, excavators, and other heavy equipment. Many of his inventions were years ahead of their time. Some are still in use today! Mr. LeTourneau became known worldwide by his nickname. Put the numbered letters into the puzzle grid to discover what it was!

15-M 11-A 3-E 2-H 6-A
19-N 17-V 10-E 4-D

1	2	3	█	4	5	6	7	█	8	9
10	11	12	13	14	15	16	17	18	19	20

12-R 8-O 16-O 1-T 18-I 9-F 5-E 7-N 14-H 20-G 13-T

WHAT IS IT?

Add the missing lines and collect the letters in the maze to find the name for this mighty earth mover.

What do you get when you take a

CRAWLER TRACTOR

and add a

BLADE

to the front?

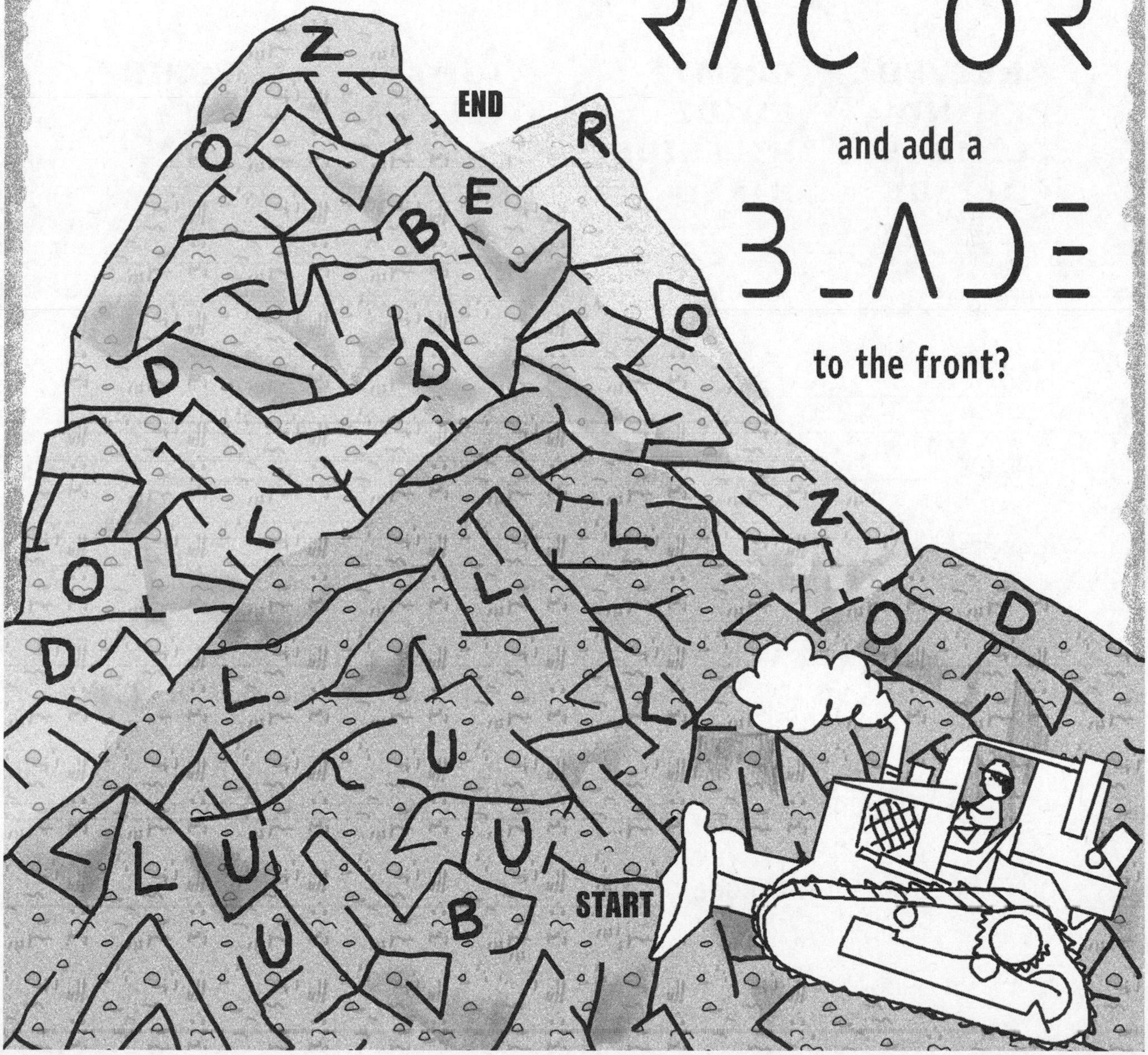

END

START

47

EYES EVERYWHERE

If you are operating heavy equipment, you have to look, listen, and be aware of everything that is going on around you. Otherwise, someone is likely to get hurt—maybe even killed!

Using the word list, fill in the blanks to complete the story. Each word fits in only one place. Then look for all the words in the letter grid on the next page. The long "I" sound in each word is represented by an "EYE." Remember to keep your eyes open on the job!

ARRIVED   GRIMY   MIGHTY   SUNSHINE
BEHIND   GUIDE   OVERTIME
CLIMBED   HILLSIDE   PERSPIRE
COLLIDE   HIRED   PRECISE

Sam was _____ to operate the hydraulic excavator.

He _____ early and _____ into the cab.

Sitting _____ the controls, Sam used _____

movements to safely _____ the _____ excavator

toward the _____. He did not _____

with anything, which is very good! The _____ was so

warm, that Sam began to _____. He felt _____,

but there was a lot more digging to do. In fact, he ended up

working _____!

F D E R 👁 H K G S I 👁 S F
Q B R F W W P U U X S K P
A 👁 E Z E I 👁 Q N 👁 P W E
S F R H S J Z A S P D R R
👁 I O R 👁 S F I H F S E S
P J K A C N R W 👁 A I S P
Y E X Z E F D W N P K H 👁
W M R A R R 👁 V E D W I R
P 👁 👁 I P J P O U I J L E
K T N R Q S 👁 N Y C P L Q
A R I A G K W T P O F S A
S E W P S R H Q N L S 👁 P
E V 👁 K I G X P O L N D Z
F O W R 👁 Z R K P 👁 R E J
C L 👁 M B E D W I D K W P
Q F S O R W P 👁 R E A S F

HALF OR WHOLE?

Guess the words defined below. Write your answers on the numbered dashes, then transfer each letter to its numbered square in the grid. Work between the grid and the answers until you can read the silly answer to the riddle.

A. Squirrel food

$\overline{1}$ $\overline{7}$ $\overline{11}$

B. To postpone

$\overline{12}$ $\overline{4}$ $\overline{22}$ $\overline{19}$ $\overline{5}$

C. On an angel's head

$\overline{15}$ $\overline{9}$ $\overline{17}$ $\overline{2}$

D. Clouds on the ground

$\overline{18}$ $\overline{6}$ $\overline{14}$

E. Number before two

$\overline{21}$ $\overline{3}$ $\overline{23}$

F. Linked circles of metal

$\overline{8}$ $\overline{20}$ $\overline{16}$ $\overline{13}$ $\overline{10}$

One man on one backhoe can dig one hole in one day. How long would it take him to dig half a hole?

1A	2C	3E	4B		5B	6D	7A
8F	9C	10F		11A	12B	13F	14D
15C	16F	17C	18D	19B	20F	21E	22B	23E

50

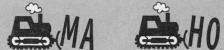  SS MA HO FO CA

 A

 I

SILLY BULLDOZERS

Each answer in this silly puzzle contains an "LL" word. Use the clues to help these bulldozers push the letter sets into the right places. Each set can be used only once, so cross them out as you use them!

 MAR

 MAR

 YE

Primary color = _ _ **L L** _ _

 PI

Campfire treat = _ _ _ _ _ _ _ _ **L L** _

 OW

Yell loudly = _ _ **L L** _ _

 TER

A sickness = _ **L L** _ _ _

 NE

Pre-butterfly = _ _ _ _ _ **L L** _ _

 ER

To walk behind = _ _ **L L** _ _

 SH

Crocodile cousin = _ **L L** _ _ _ _ _

 OR

Found at the beach = _ _ _ **L L** _

WHAT X-ACTLY ARE YOU?

Follow the directions to find out what this kind of digging machine is called!

1. Choose the word that means "to remove by digging"

   DELETE   **REMOVE**
   EXCAVATE **ERASE**

2. Remove the "E" at the end

3. Replace it with "OR"

4. Write the answer on the dotted lines

This machine is an __ __ __ __ __ __ __ __ __ .

THAT'S X-CITING!

How many Xs can you find in this picture?

52

HEAD PROTECTION

Construction workers wear hard hats to protect their heads from injury while on the site. Often you can tell their job by the color of their hat. For instance, workmen might wear yellow hard hats, but safety inspectors wear red ones! Solve the picture and letter equations to sound out some safety accessories, which can be attached to the hard hats.

1. $V + \text{(eye)} + Z + \text{(oar)}$

2. $\text{(ear)} + P + \text{(scarecrow)} - C + \text{(spider)} + TORS$

3. $M + \text{(ear)} + R$

4. $L + \text{(eye)} + \text{(tea)}$

5. $\text{(chin)} + S + \text{(mousetrap)} - \text{(mouse)}$

TIME TO GO

Safety rules say that a worker must replace a hard hat if it's been dented or broken. Hard hats must also be replaced after a few years even if they seem to be in perfect condition! Count the number of hard hats below that have the same shape on the front. Which shape appears the least number of times? This is the number of years that a worker can safely wear his or her hat before it needs to be replaced!

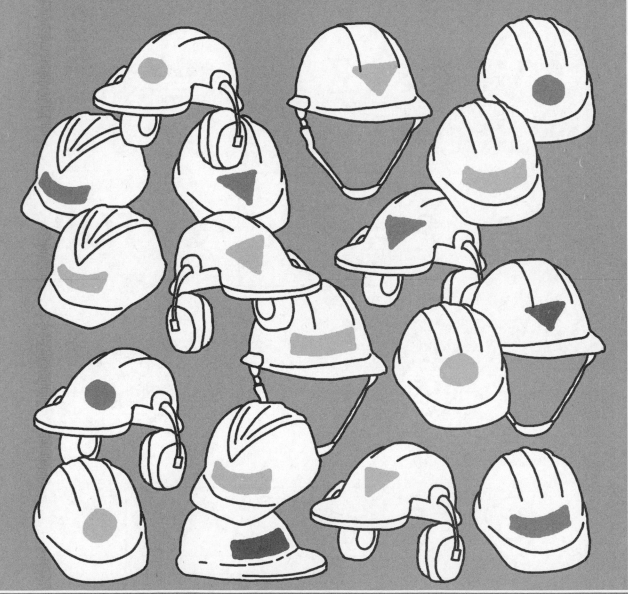

OPPOSITES

Backhoes and bulldozers are common construction vehicles that both move dirt. What's the difference between them? To find out, guess the words defined below. Write your answers in the shaded boxes.

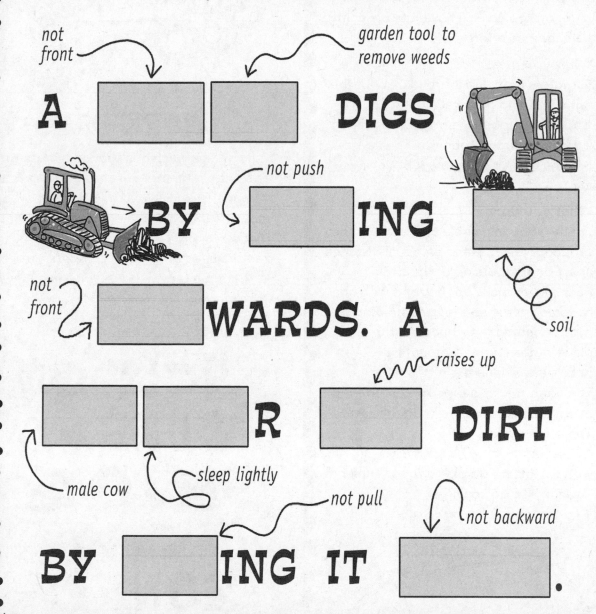

not front →

garden tool to remove weeds

A [ ] [ ] DIGS

not push

BY [ ] ING

soil

not front

[ ] WARDS. A

raises up

[ ] R [ ] DIRT

male cow

sleep lightly

not pull

not backward

BY [ ] ING IT [ ] .

TRACTOR PULL

A tractor pull is a competition to see which vehicle can pull the heaviest load the farthest. Test your strength in this game where you are the tractor! Play inside or outside, but be sure to have lots of room and an adult as referee.

What you need:

- 3 tractors (you and 2 friends) about the same size and physical ability
- 1 adult to supervise and be the referee
- 3 yards of strong rope
- 3 items to pick up (caps, rubber rings, etc.)

What you do:

- Tie the rope in a circle and lay it on the ground. Players stand an equal distance apart on the outside of the circle.
- Each player picks up the rope with one hand and turns so the hand holding the rope is behind their back. All three players stretch the rope until it becomes a triangle.
- The adult places a pick-up item in front of each player, just out of their reach. The adult signals GO!
- All players try to pick up their item without letting go of the rope. The first "tractor" to do so wins!

WORK DAYS

Many of the machines used in a modern tractor pull are more like drag racers than tractors! They are loud and flashy, have sponsors, popular drivers, and crazy fans. That's a far cry from the working farm tractors used in the first competition of 1929. At that time they had a saying that showed tractors were used more for work than fun. Break the Flip-Flop code to see what it was!

PLAY ON
SUNDAY,
PLOW
ON
MONDAY.

CHAPTER 5
MIXERS AND SHAKERS

RAT-A-TAT-TAT

What happens if a cement mixer breaks down while driving to a job? Start at the letter marked with a dot. Read around the border to find out!

READY MADE

These trucks bring freshly mixed concrete directly to a construction site. The concrete is mixed while the trucks travel, and is ready to use when they arrive!

Unscramble the words in these mixers to see what ingredients generally go into making concrete.

FUN FACT
The first "transit mixer" was used in 1916!

58

BACK END

Some concrete mixers unload from the front end. They need only one person to drive and release the concrete down the chute. Other mixers unload from the back end. These vehicles need both a driver and a chute man. Look at the letters sliding down the chute and across the ground. What letter does each one follow in the alphabet? Change all the letters and you will know the nickname for this second kind of mixer.

C V U U E V N Q F S

MIX IT UP

The words in the list all mean "mix." Can you find them in the letter grid?

UNITE, INTEGRATE, SCRAMBLE, BLEND, MERGE, DILUTE, MINGLE, COMBINE

```
N E L B M A R C S
S C R M B K U O W H D I
U N I T E I M E R G E I E R
M I T E T S I F D I T O T D C
E C O M B I N E I A M T A I O
U T E F O G O L D E E R L M
R A D I L U T E R P G E R
C O L E G O C O M E O D
M R G E O T N T E M
C O B L E N D
I M
```

HARD STUFF

Concrete doesn't start out rock hard, it just dries that way. When it is first used, concrete needs to be workable until it is in its final shape. Each project, however, requires a different consistency. For instance, roadways need very stiff concrete, but walls must have a more fluid concrete.

A special word is used to describe how stiff the concrete is before it hardens. To discover that term, follow the line from each picture at the top of this puzzle to a box at the bottom. Write the first letter of the picture into the box, then read the boxes from left to right.

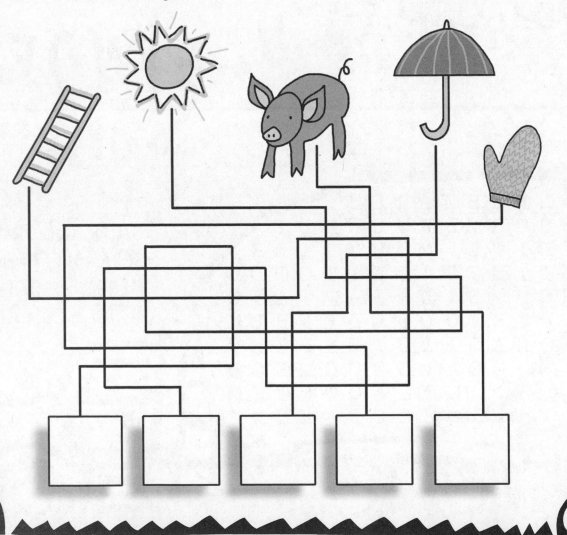

STEP BY STEP

Number these pictures of the patio project from the start to the finish!

SILLY SENTENCES

One letter is needed to finish each of these silly sentences about this road crew.

__arry __eaved __is __eavy __ydraulic __ammer.

__onald __ecklessly __olled __ight.

__erry's __ackhammer __ust __umped.

__arl's __oncrete __racked __rookedly.

__ike's __ixer __ade __arvelous __ud.

WORD MERGE

This mixer is not making concrete. It is mixing other things. In each of these letter sets, two words have been mixed together. Use the clues to help you separate them!

Two colors = **ORYEANLLGEOW**

Two animals = **ELEMONPHAKENTY**

Two numbers = **FELOUREVETENEN**

Two states = **WIDISCAONHOSIN**

Two fruits = **CHAPERRPLIEESS**

Two flowers = **DACAFRNAFTOIDILON**

GOOD VIBRATIONS

If you shake the word V-I-B-R-A-T-I-O-N-S how many smaller words will fall out? Try to make 35 words that use at least two letters. Extra Challenge: Don't use the letter "S" to make plurals. Extra Extra Challenge: How many five-letter words can you make?

1. _____ 8. _____ 15. _____ 22. _____ 29. _____
2. _____ 9. _____ 16. _____ 23. _____ 30. _____
3. _____ 10. _____ 17. _____ 24. _____ 31. _____
4. _____ 11. _____ 18. _____ 25. _____ 32. _____
5. _____ 12. _____ 19. _____ 26. _____ 33. _____
6. _____ 13. _____ 20. _____ 27. _____ 34. _____
7. _____ 14. _____ 21. _____ 28. _____ 35. _____

DANGEROUS NOISE

Machines that mix, vibrate, and pound make noises that are dangerously loud. How can operators protect their hearing? To find out, break the Vowel Switch code and connect the dots.

**THUY WUIR
SIFUTY
UIRMEFFS**

63

POUND THE GROUND

A jackhammer is a portable drill powered by compressed air. It is used to break up concrete and asphalt. A jackhammer does the same job as a man swinging a pickax, only much more easily. How much faster can the machine go than the man? To find out, fill in the empty boxes with the answers to the equations!

AN EXPERIENCED WORKER CAN SWING A PICKAX

[ ] TIMES A MINUTE

dozen x dozen -134

A JACKHAMMER CAN POUND THE GROUND ABOUT

[ ] TIMES A MINUTE

days in a year -215

J IS FOR JACKHAMMER

Each of the clues defines a word that starts with the letter "J." See how many of them you know, then try to fit all the answers into the crisscross grid on the facing page.

ACROSS

2. Prison
3. First month
4. Denim pants
6. Small chewy candy in many flavors
7. Glass container with screw top
10. Person in charge of the courtroom
12. Necklaces and bracelets
15. A long trip
16. Largest planet
17. Lively Irish dance

DOWN

1. Tropical forest
2. He/she keeps schools clean
4. Broken old stuff
5. Being envious
7. Keep 3 balls in the air
8. Horse's rider in a race
9. Large spotted wild cat
10. What someone does for work
11. Squishy sea creature
12. Lightweight coat
13. Funny card in a deck
14. Small car of the army
16. Fast airplane

Can you think of a bird with a head like a jackhammer?

Break the vowel switch code to find out!

65

AWAY IT GOES

A conveyor truck looks like a dump truck, but has a conveyor belt built in. The rock or dirt is automatically unloaded onto the moving belt, and can be thrown in a fine stream up to 18 feet away, in almost any direction! The operator wears a control panel and directs the stream of material using a joystick.

Figure out what number is missing from each path so that it adds up to the number in the hole. The path that is missing the most is the one the operator will use first!

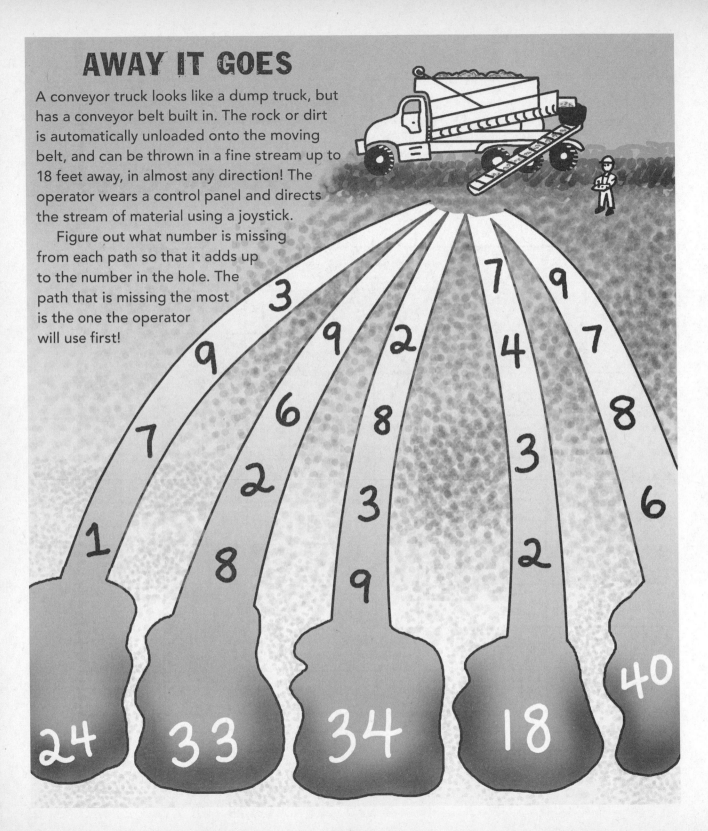

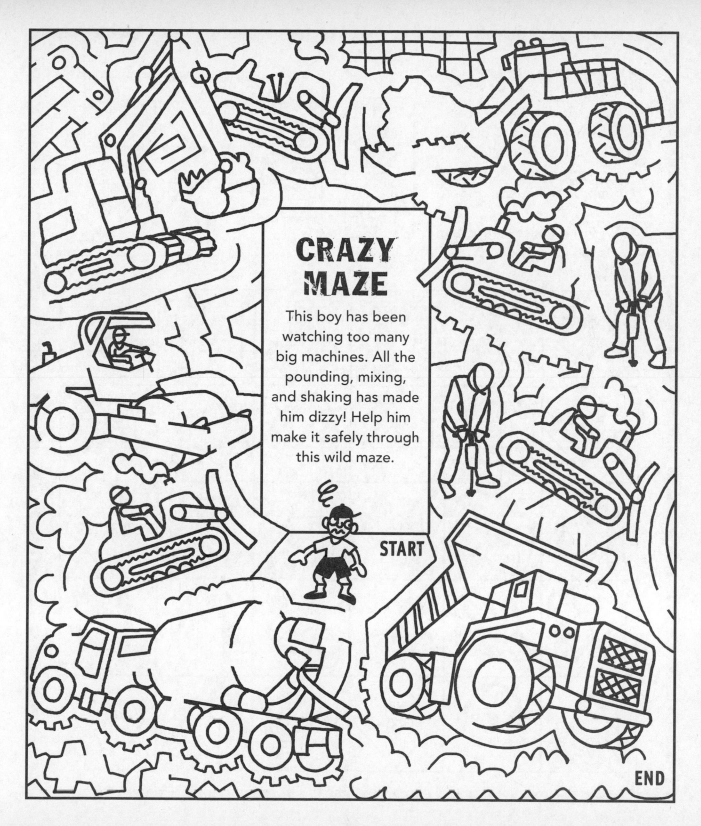

CRAZY MAZE

This boy has been watching too many big machines. All the pounding, mixing, and shaking has made him dizzy! Help him make it safely through this wild maze.

START

END

SAFETY FIRST

Construction workers wear and use many items to protect themselves on the job. Find these four picture groups in the puzzle grid.

EXTRA FUN: Which safety item appears only once?

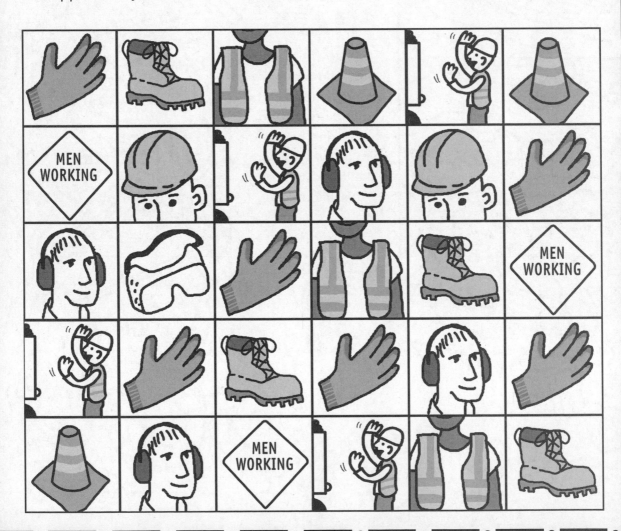

CHAPTER 6
ROLLERS AND POUNDERS

SHAKE, RATTLE . . .

Before a road-paving crew can put down a layer of hot tar, the dirt under the road must be pounded flat and hard. That's a job for the vibratory drum compactor. It doesn't look very powerful—what is the secret inside this piece of equipment? Break the Reverse Squash code to find out!

HEAVY WEIGHTS INSIDE
THE ROLLING DRUM SLAM
DOWN CAUSING POWERFUL
VIBRATIONS THAT PACK
DIRT DOWN TIGHT.

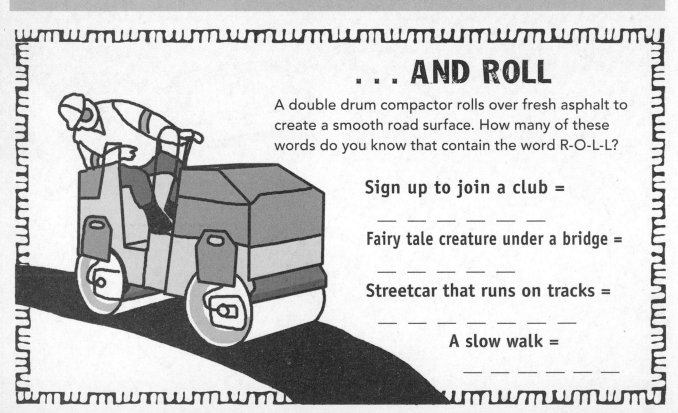

. . . AND ROLL

A double drum compactor rolls over fresh asphalt to create a smooth road surface. How many of these words do you know that contain the word R-O-L-L?

Sign up to join a club =

_ _ _ _ _ _

Fairy tale creature under a bridge =

_ _ _ _ _

Streetcar that runs on tracks =

_ _ _ _ _ _

A slow walk =

_ _ _ _ _ _

WHAT IF . . .

Fill in all the spaces that contain the letters F-L-A-T to find the silly answer.

What if Hollywood made a movie about the battle between two paving machines? What would they call it?

DUMB CLUCK

There is a word hiding in each row across this puzzle, and each of them is missing a letter! Write the loose letters from the bottom of the page into the empty boxes to complete the hidden words. Circle or highlight the words you make. When you read them from top to bottom, they will form the silly answer to the riddle.
Hint: All letters will be used only once.

Why did the road cross the chicken?

S A T ☐ E N D

C H I ☐ K E N

F E W ☐ I D P

B N O ☐ R E D

U D G ☐ T V E

W I N ☐ U T A

Q L O ☐ R Y L

A T H ☐ M O N

V P A ☐ E R S

C O W ☐ Y O U

HEY!

T
H E F E D
C A O V

SQUASH IT FLAT

A landfill has to fit in as much trash as possible. Special bulldozers called landfill compactors are used to spread out the garbage and squash the trash pile flat. To do this, the dozers are extra heavy. A "small" one can weigh over 80,000 pounds—more than four big school buses! Add giant metal wheels covered with seven-inch steel cleats, and you have some serious squashing power. See if you can recognize the ten items this compactor has flattened today.

HOT WORKER, COOL WORKER

Construction workers and road crews often work outside on blazing hot summer days. It is almost impossible for them to get cool on the job! Make a path for this sweaty hot worker so he is cool and comfortable at the end. You must alternate a hot face with a cool face. You can move up and down, or side-to-side, but not diagonally. If you come to a sunburned or freezing driver, you are going the wrong way!

Fun Fact: Road paving crews try to work at night because there is less traffic, but also because it is much cooler!

BIG BREAKER

The hydraulic breaker is a powerful kind of hammer used to quickly demolish rocks or concrete. This tool attaches to an excavator's arm so it can reach all kinds of places! To learn the nickname for this big breaker, solve this puzzle. Each clue suggests a word. Write the answers in the spaces provided. When you are finished, read the shaded spaces.

1. Not goodbye
2. First number
3. Hear with this
4. Money to landlord
5. Biggest brass horn
6. Wake up clock

Hint: The last letter of one word is the first letter of the next!

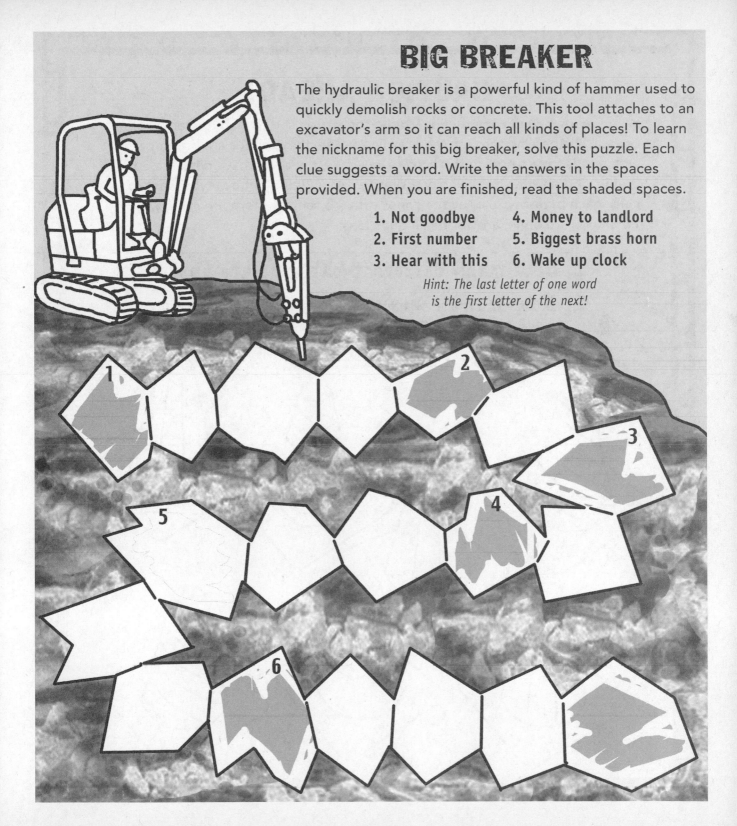

75

CAUTION AHEAD!

When there is road construction, traffic cones are used to warn drivers to slow down while passing through the area. In real life, these cones are bright orange with a reflective stripe. In this activity, however, the cones have patterns on them—and you decide the colors! What you do: Figure out how you want to color each pattern. Color all the cones with the same pattern the same way. When you are done, answer these questions:

1. How many different patterns are there?
2. How many cones are in each pattern?
3. Do any patterns have just one?

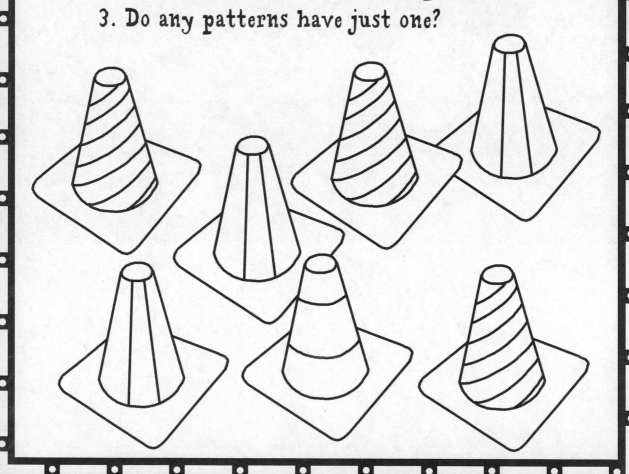

PICK A PILE

In construction work, a pile is a long, slender column that is driven into the ground as a foundation for a building. Solve the picture and word equations to sound out what three materials are used to make piles.

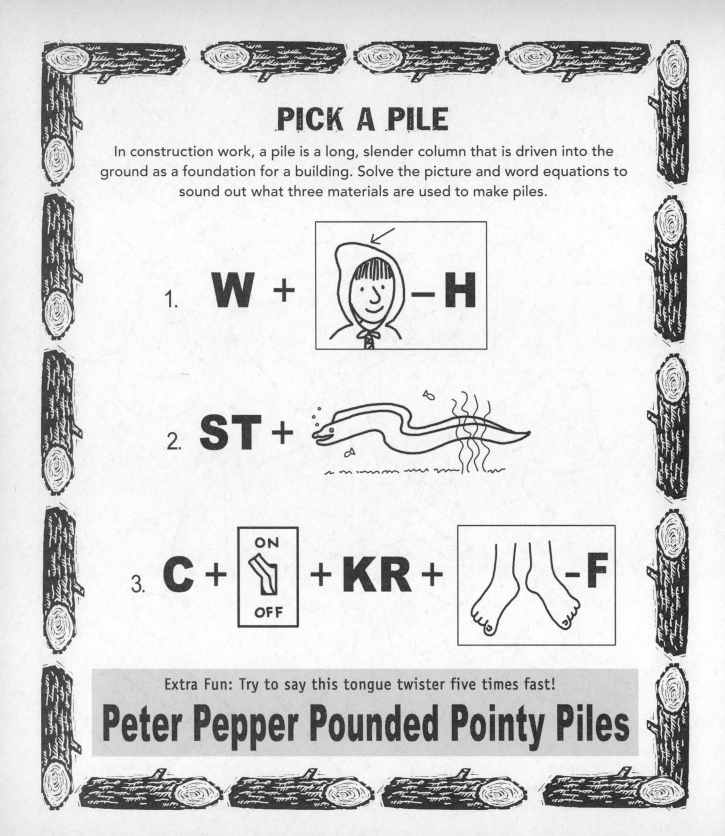

Pile 1: Choose even numbers

68	70	72
56	67	69
51	50	49
52	54	44
47	42	46
38	43	45
35	32	31
34	30	33
27	25	26
21	28	22
24	20	23
19	15	16

GOING DOWN

Pile drivers are placed over a pile with a crane. Then, a weight is repeatedly lifted high to the top of the pile driver, and dropped onto the pile. The pounding forces the pile into the ground. See if you can pound your way from top to bottom of each puzzle!

- Follow the direction at the top of each pile.
- Start at the top left-hand corner.
- End up at the bottom right-hand corner.
- The numbers must steadily decrease as you work your way down!

Pile 2: Choose numbers divisible by 3

99	90	88
98	96	97
95	94	90
92	91	87
86	75	74
88	70	69
71	60	55
58	54	61
56	53	51
43	44	42
31	28	30
19	20	21

BOOM! BOOM! BOOM! BOOM!

Driving in piles can be a really noisy job! Color in the four times that B-O-O-M is spelled correctly.

```
B O M O O M
O B O M B O
M O B B M O
B B B O O M
O M M O B B
M B O O O M
B O M O B M
M O O B B
B O O M O O
O O M B O B
B O B O M O
O M M O O O
M B O O M O
M O B M O M
```

SHAKE IT DOWN

A hammer usually works by pounding down onto something, like a hammer driving a nail into a board. Instead of pounding, a vibratory pile hammer shakes the piles to force them into the ground. They are often chosen when construction is very close to other buildings. Break the Plus Two code to learn why!

RFCW YPC
JCQQ LMGQW

Hmmm... That's weird!

CHAPTER 7
DRILLERS AND CUTTERS

VERY BORING

Some construction projects use a gigantic drill to bore through rock. The cutterhead on these powerful machines is usually from 6 to 36 feet in diameter, but at least one drill in the world is 50 feet across! What the heck does this machine make? Follow the directions to find out!

Each clue suggests a five-letter word ending with "L."

Write each word into the puzzle from the outer edge to the center.

Read the letters in the outer ring.

1. Use this to dry off

2. Normal

3. A fiction book

4. Bellybutton

5. Same as

6. True to a friend

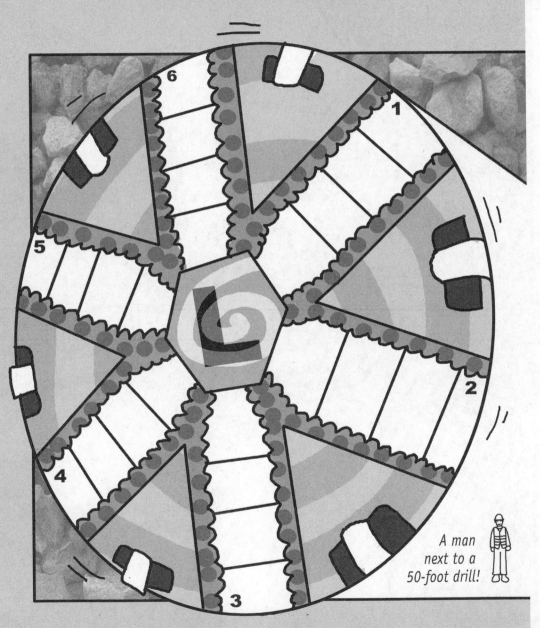

A man next to a 50-foot drill!

82

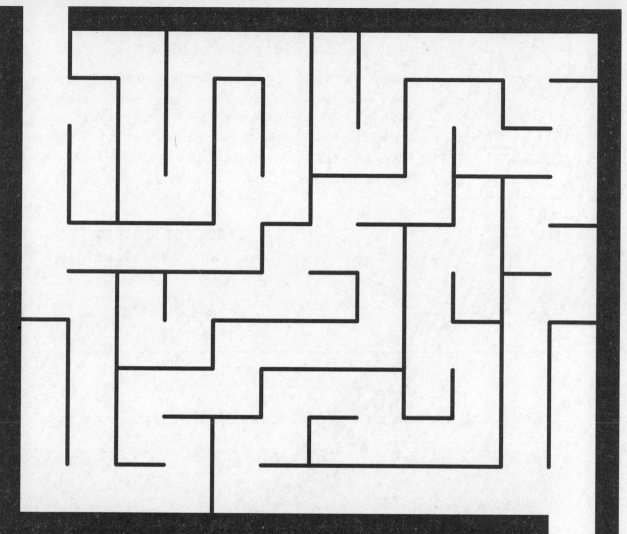

HIGH AND LOW

The vehicles and other heavy equipment used deep in coal mines are specialized versions of their cousins above ground. Up top, the driver of a giant dump truck will haul coal while sitting in a cab 20 feet in the air. Down below, the driver of a coal shuttle will be sitting just 2 feet above the tunnel floor. Sometimes the mine is so low that a shuttle driver has to lie down while he is driving! Help this coal shuttle wind its way up to the surface to unload.

MAKE A DITCH

The machines built for cutting ditches can save time, money, and a lot of backaches. They look like giant chainsaws and can quickly create a ditch the right size for pipes or cables. Sometimes this machine has a blade that is up to 5 feet wide. These are used to make a ditch 20 feet deep! Follow the directions to discover the name of this handy machine.

- Add one letter to finish the last word of each sentence.

- Read the letters in the ditch from top to bottom.

Dogs wag their... ___ A I L S

Cattle live on a... ___ A N C H

Another word for "foe" is... ___ N E M Y

The opposite of day is... ___ I G H T

Several people can sit on a... ___ O U C H

You greet someone by saying... ___ E L L O

Two numbers that are the same are... ___ Q U A L

A natural stream of water is a... ___ I V E R

84

AHHH! GRRR!

Some construction projects use a large screw with a wide, deep thread. As it turns into the earth, it fills with dirt. The screw is then lifted, cleared, and re-lowered into the hole. Its job is to cut holes for pipes or foundation piles. What is its name? Start at the top of the screw and read every other letter as you twist your way down into the ground. Extra fun: Start at the second letter of the screw and read every other letter to get another name for this tool!

HA HA

What grows larger the more you take away? Look at this page in a mirror and read the answer from the bottom up!

HOLE HA HA

STREET SCRAMBLE

A road cutter is a powerful circular saw that cuts through concrete and asphalt. In this puzzle, a cutter has gone crazy and has cut up a portion of the street that wasn't empty! Copy the pattern from each box into the grid to see what items lay in its path.

2A

3B

1B

3C

1C

3A

2B

2C

1A

A   B   C

1

2

3

86

HURRY HARVESTER

A tree harvester is a type of excavator with a special harvesting head attached to the hydraulic arm. This device can grip a tree, saw it down, strip off the bark, and cut the tree into preset lengths. How quickly can it do all four tasks?

Take out the extra letters hidden in these tree trunks, then read the trunks in order.

1. NNINNNTNNN

2. TRARKRERSR

3. AALEASASAA

4. GTGHGAGNG

5. ETHEIRTEYE

6. SBECBONDBS

CUT & DRILL

Use a yellow marker to highlight words in the list that mean "to cut off."
Use a green marker to highlight words in the list that mean "to drill into."
Then find all 21 of these words in the grid. Remember, words can be found
in any direction, including diagonally!

AMPUTATE
BORE
BUTCHER
CARVE
CHOP
CLIP
DISSECT
PENETRATE
PIERCE
PRUNE
PUNCTURE
SAW
SEVER
SHAVE
SHEAR
SLASH
SLICE
SLIT
SNIP
SPLIT
TRIM

```
H A P R U U T E O R B A M P P M
C A R V E N N S L I O C E T I T
S M L A S U H D I C R U R L D
P P P B R P D I S S E C T O C I
I U I P B A M I H L E V C A M S
A T E I C A R B E I B D I H I E
M A S E P I E R A P U I R F O T
P T P P E N E T R A T E A M M P
I E I B P R U P S N C A C E L I
B N L O S R A U C H H P U C N T
S O S S L C N N Y S E V E R T A
B S T L T E P C S I R P C E T M
C H X I A O R T L C A R V I Y P
A A L C N S U U C P O A L P O W
R S S E B O H R I U H P S L A R
C V S H A E V E T S S L I S D Y
```

88

ZAPPY ZIPPER

An asphalt zipper is a handy machine that easily attaches to a backhoe or loader. It grinds up old asphalt, which is used to fix potholes and old parking lots, and for other street repairs.

Move just one letter of each word to make a whole new word! Hint: We gave you a clue for the new word.

EACH _____
dull pain

BELOW _____
arm joint

BLOW _____
cereal holder

ODOR _____
house exit

LEAF _____
dog biter

TONES _____
rock

ROAD REPAIR

Before the zipper was invented, old asphalt had to be cut into sections, peeled up, and hauled away. Now, instead of ending up in a landfill, the existing materials are reused. Start at the "R" and follow the arrows to find another word for this process.

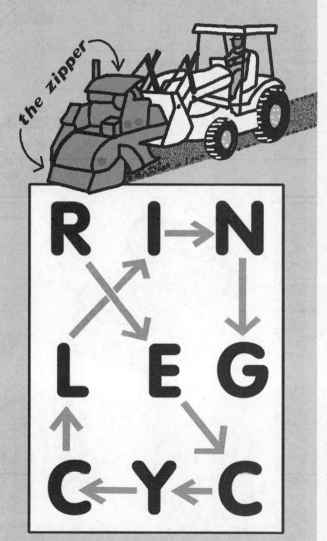

the zipper

R   I → N

L   E   G

C ← Y ← C

STUMPED

Each of these stumps has a number that represents how many minutes it will take the stump grinder to chew through it. Figure out how many hours the operator should plan to spend grinding this whole field!

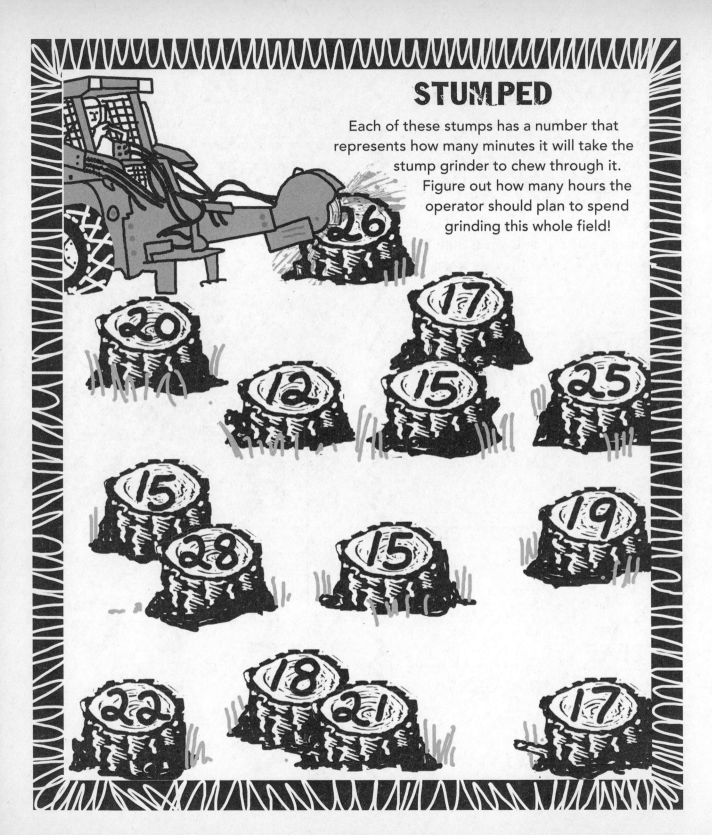

WHAT A WALL!

How do you build a tunnel underneath a big city without having the buildings and roads above collapse into the hole? The city of Boston, Massachusetts had to figure this out when they started a project called "The Big Dig." Engineers decided to build temporary structures called slurry walls to support the city while they worked. These reinforced concrete walls reach from the surface all the way down to hard and stable bedrock. Follow the directions to learn an amazing fact about slurry walls and The Big Dig!

   Place each of the letters in one of the empty boxes beneath it. The letters stay in the same column, but not in the same order. Hint: We left some letters in place for you!

A				E										
I	A			O			C					I	F	
S	N	S	F	S			M	A	Z			H	E	
W	L	U	E	H	E		N	A	E		S	R	H	
E	O	U	T	D	Y	L	I	I	G	Y	U	H	G	
R	N	T	S	R	E	I	W	N	L	Y	N	O	E	E
			T				B				D			
			R	R					L	L				
	C							K			T			
		L	L						Y	O				
H	O				,		O						T	
		T	I						I	T				
B					N		W		S		T			
	O	O					A		A		I		G	!

HOLEY SCHMOLEY!

A rotary blast drill typically makes a series of holes an equal distance apart over a particular area of ground. What are the holes for? To find out, make a path from START to END. Each new box you travel to should have one more filled circle than the box before. When you have finished, read the letters in order along the path.

Want to be a blast drill operator?
Here's part of the job description: The drill operator must correctly operate the rotary drill to prevent plugged bits, bent steel, and collapsed holes; The position requires regular attendance on rotating 12-hour shifts. Must have the ability to hear backup alarms.

START	P	L
E	X	O
V	I	S
E	S	END

USEFUL UTILITIES

Our homes use many utilities to keep our lights and heat on, showers running, stoves cooking, and computers, televisions, and phones connected. When things go wrong, a serviceman needs to be called!

In this code, each tool represents one of two letters. Figure out which one is needed to complete the names of the five utility companies that might come to make repairs.

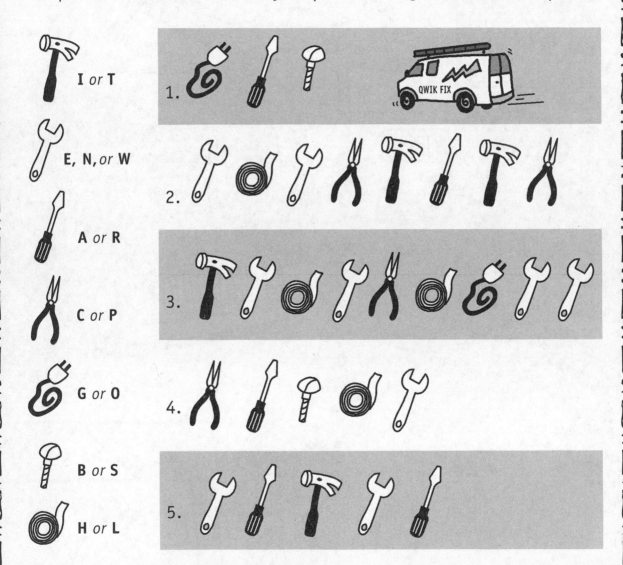

I *or* T

E, N, *or* W

A *or* R

C *or* P

G *or* O

B *or* S

H *or* L

QWIK FIX

PICKY, PICKY

Cherry pickers are mechanical arms that quickly lift utility workers up to fix things located high on phone or power poles. This electrician is going to pick the sneakers off the phone wires. Add the points to see which wire gives him the highest score!

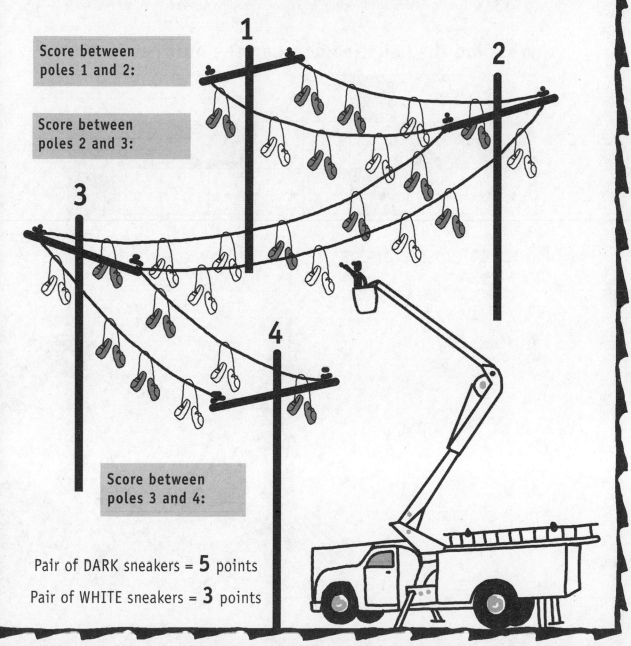

Score between poles 1 and 2:

Score between poles 2 and 3:

Score between poles 3 and 4:

Pair of DARK sneakers = **5** points

Pair of WHITE sneakers = **3** points

HELP IS ON THE WAY

Guess the words defined below. Write your answers on the numbered dashes, then transfer each letter to its numbered square in the grid. Work between the grid and the answers until you can read the silly answer to the riddle!

What did the ballerina do when she hurt her foot?

1	2	3		4	5	6	7	8	9
			10	11	12				
13	14	15		16	17	18	19	20	!

A. Money to cross a bridge

$\overline{10}$ $\overline{14}$ $\overline{7}$ $\overline{6}$

B. Hot road covering

$\overline{16}$ $\overline{5}$ $\overline{17}$

C. Side of your face

$\overline{19}$ $\overline{2}$ $\overline{12}$ $\overline{8}$ $\overline{20}$

D. Small storage building

$\overline{1}$ $\overline{11}$ $\overline{3}$ $\overline{9}$

E. How a baby looks

$\overline{4}$ $\overline{18}$ $\overline{13}$ $\overline{15}$

Please, hurry!

Don't worry — almost done!

FAST FIXERS

A big storm has passed through the town and services have been interrupted. The gas, electric, and cable companies have been called. Which utility truck will reach the Blairs' home first? Place a 1, 2, or 3 in the trucks to show the order in which they arrived.

 The electric company has promised a repairman in one hour.

 The gas company is 30 miles away. A repairman will drive 60 miles an hour to the Blairs' house.

 The cable repairman is in the neighborhood, but is working at another house. He will be available in 45 minutes.

GAS LEAK

Someone smelled a gas leak, and called the gas company. They are sending a repairman to check it out. He found five words that each contain the word G-A-S. Can you?

Long stories = __ __ __ __ __

Sudden breath = __ __ __ __

A deep cut = __ __ __ __

Roman garments = __ __ __ __ __

White whales = __ __ __ __ __ __ __

PATCHING POTHOLES

Potholes are holes in the road caused when chunks of the roadway break away. They can become deep and cause damage to cars that do not avoid them! Help the road crew work their way over and under through the maze, patching the potholes along the way.

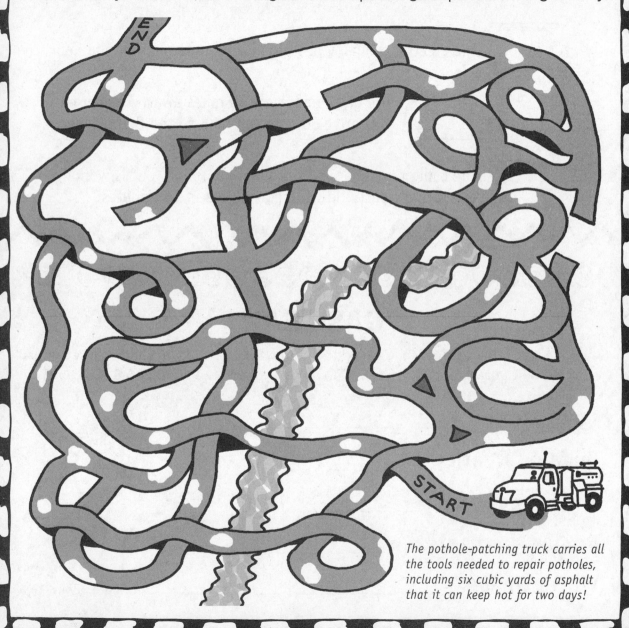

The pothole-patching truck carries all the tools needed to repair potholes, including six cubic yards of asphalt that it can keep hot for two days!

THANKS, COOKIE

Kevin and his mom baked sugar cookies to say "Thank you!" to the road crew that helped their neighborhood during a big storm. All the cookies on the cooling rack came from one of the rolled-out batches of dough. Can you figure out which one?

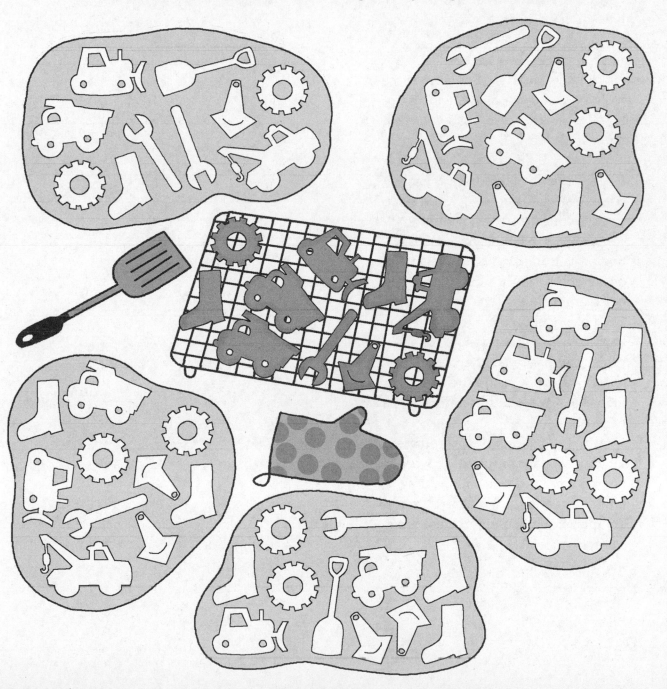

SUPER SCAFFOLDING

A scaffold is a platform on which construction workers stand while they work on the side of a building. Sometimes only a few sections of scaffolding are needed. Sometimes the scaffolding can cover a whole building! Follow the directions to build your own super scaffolding.

- Play this game with a friend. Each player uses a different colored pencil to try to build the most scaffolding.
- Taking turns, each player connects two neighboring dots. The line can go up and down or side-to-side, but not diagonally.
- Each player should try to be the one to draw a line that closes a square. When that happens, the player makes a large X inside the box. This means a new piece of scaffolding has been completed!
- Continue playing until each puzzle-building grid is completely covered, or start near the bottom and play until the scaffolding reaches the top. The player who completes the most scaffolding wins!

In the Guinness World Records, the tallest freestanding scaffolding is listed at 320 feet. This scaffolding wasn't around an ordinary building—it was to help workers restore the Statue of Liberty!

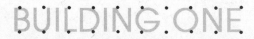

BUILDING ONE

100

BUILDING TWO   BUILDING THREE

FLOODING FOOLERY

A water main pipe has broken and caused a flood. It has washed away one word and replaced it with another word that rhymes. Can you figure out all the changes?

Teddy into an autumn fruit

_ _ _ _ _ to _ _ _ _

Shellfish into a baby sheep

_ _ _ _ _ to _ _ _ _

Wooden box into a dish

_ _ _ _ _ to _ _ _ _ _

Small stream into seven days

_ _ _ _ _ _ to _ _ _ _

Dried fruit into a small branch

_ _ _ _ to _ _ _ _

Sleeveless shirt into a visitor

_ _ _ _ to _ _ _ _

DRAIN DEBRIS

Storm drains are designed to collect surface water after heavy rain and reduce flooding. Because they also collect debris and other pollutants, they must be cleaned regularly. A vacuum/flush combination truck will clean, haul, and dispose of debris so that public waterways do not get contaminated.

Follow the directions and cross off the words described. When you have finished, you will know another name for a storm drain.

Cross off any words that:

- start with the letter D
- mean the same as STORM
- include the letters EA
- rhyme with WASTE
- end in the letter T

DITCH	CATCH	REACH	DIRT
LEAKS	DEBRIS	HASTE	GALE
FLOOD	PIT	BASIN	WET
DEEP	CLEAN	HURRICANE	TASTE
BASTE	LEAVES	DRIPS	FLOAT

WHAT AM I?

Add the missing lines and connect the dots to find the answer to the rhyming riddle!

When trash collects, I make things neat.
It is my job to come and sweep.
My brooms will spin, my water sprays.
I work to clean throughout the days.

STREET SWEEPER

CHAPTER 9

DESTROYERS AND DEMOLISHERS

SOMETHING TO NOTHING

Sometimes one structure needs to be removed before a new one is built in the same place. Number these pictures in a logical order to show the demolition process.

ALL CLEAR

Before a structure can be demolished, a thorough check is done from top to bottom to make sure that no one is in the building!

START

Start in the attic and work your way through the house. You must find a path through each room, including the front porch and the basement!

END

SPECTATORS AT THE SITE

A crowd has gathered to watch the demolition crew at work. They have brought big signs with them. Are they protesters or supporters? Fill in the blocks on the signs according to the directions to find out!

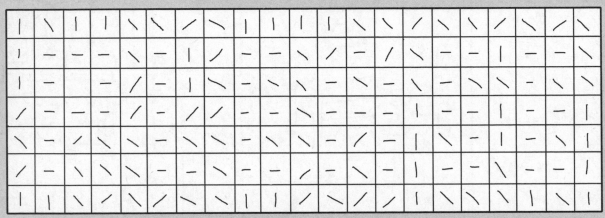

Fill in all the squares with a horizontal line.

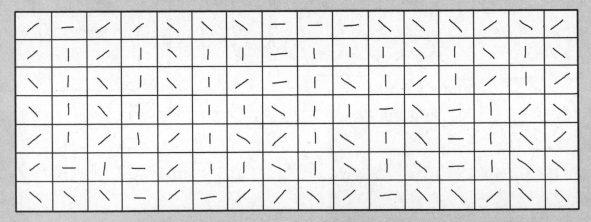

Fill in all the squares with a vertical line.

Fill in all the boxes with
a dot in the center.

Fill in all the boxes with a dot on the left.

GET A GRIP

A demolition excavator can take a building down bite by bite. Designed to be extra tough, these machines have a bucket with a powerful gripping thumb. Instead of just scooping, this excavator can grip and pull. How many hours will it take to demolish this bunch of abandoned buildings? Count up the three different shapes. Use the point system to find out the total number of minutes it will take, and divide by 60!

Hint: Only count the shapes in the white buildings.

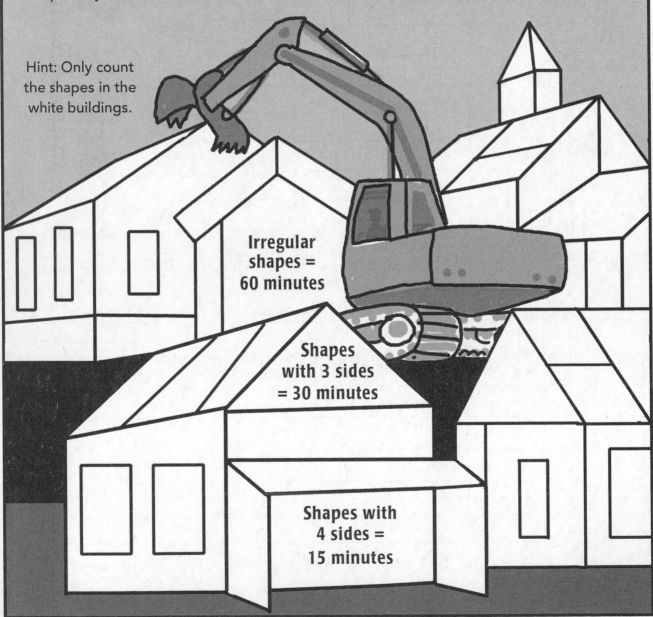

Irregular shapes = 60 minutes

Shapes with 3 sides = 30 minutes

Shapes with 4 sides = 15 minutes

DY-NO-MITE!

Explosives are used to destroy old buildings—particularly for one type of demolition. Crack the Number Substitution code in these sticks of dynamite to see when explosives are chosen.

WHAT A WRECK!

The wrecking ball is one of the earliest demolition tools ever used. It is smashed repeatedly against a wall or building until it is destroyed. This makes a lot of noise! See if you can find all twelve noisy words hidden in the wrecking ball.

SMASH, CRASH, BOOM, CRACK, BASH, BAM, SLAM, SMACK, BANG, POW, KABOOM, THUD

HELPING HANDS

Excavators and backhoes are handy machines to have around when you are building something new. They are also amazing tools for when you need to demolish an old building! Just pop off the bucket and hook up one of these heavy-duty attachments. Put the number of each attachment on the dash in front of its name.

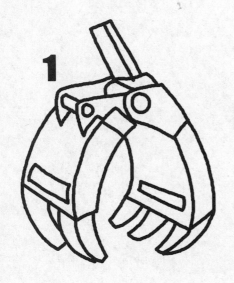

___Clearing Rake

___Concrete Pulverizer

___Grapple

___Metal Shears

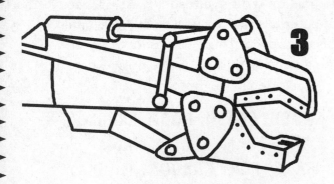

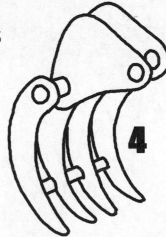

CRAZY CLOSE-UPS

Someone tried to take pictures at the construction site, but zoomed in a bit too close. Can you tell what he was looking at in each photo?

SUPER SUCTION

A vactor is a very powerful vacuum cleaner. It can suck up all kinds of debris, including rocks and mud. When is a vactor used? To find out, copy the patterns from the puzzle pieces into the empty puzzle grid.

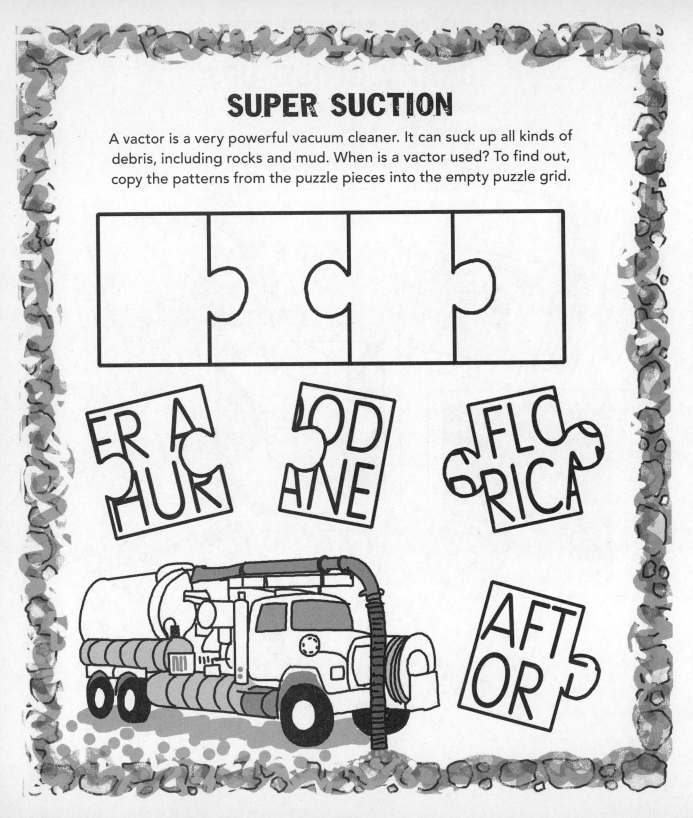

DANGER DUDE

Look at the tires below. Some look like they are linked through each other. Others look like tires that overlap but are not linked. Cross out the letter pairs on the tires that are linked. Read the remaining letters in the unlinked tires from left to right and top to bottom to get the silly answer to the joke!

What part of the dump truck causes the most accidents at a demolition site?

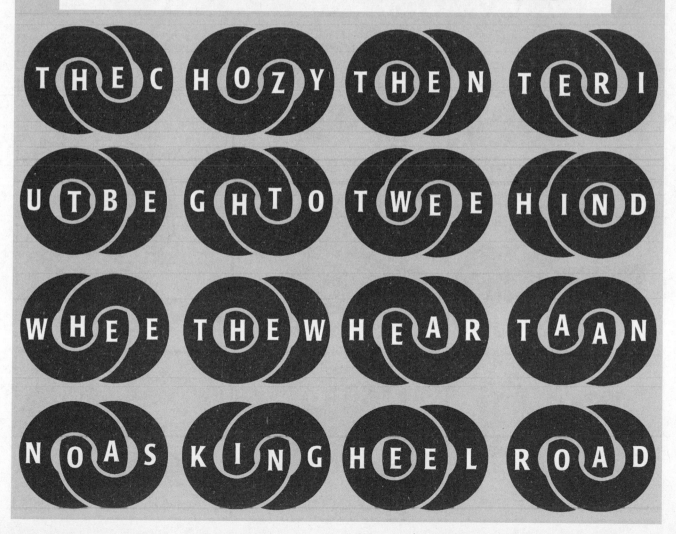

THE C　　HOZY　　THEN　　TERI

UTBE　　GHTOT　　WEE　　HIND

WHEE　　THEW　　HEAR　　TAAN

NOAS　　KING　　HEEL　　ROAD

115

BEEP BEEP BINGO

This is a great game for a long car ride. Be sure to use a pencil so you can erase your marks from the bingo card and play again.

1. Look for the dump trucks, bulldozers, and other construction vehicles pictured. When you spot one, put a light X in the corner of that box.
2. To get BINGO you need a straight line of Xs across the board in any direction, including diagonally.
   - Extra Points: If you see one of the trucks backing up, you get 2 extra points!
   - Extra Fun: If you're traveling with a friend or sibling, you can share the gameboard by using your initials in different corners of the picture boxes.

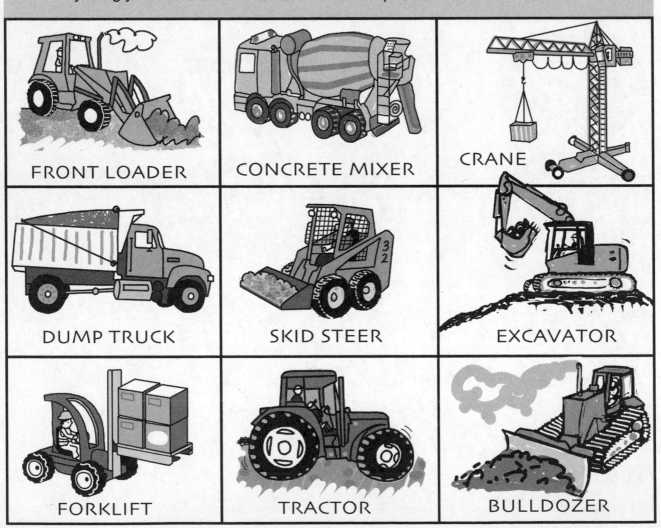

FRONT LOADER	CONCRETE MIXER	CRANE
DUMP TRUCK	SKID STEER	EXCAVATOR
FORKLIFT	TRACTOR	BULLDOZER

LOOK AGAIN!

Find these picture pieces in this book. Write the name of the puzzle each piece is from in the space under each box. Hint: There is only one piece from each chapter!

1.

2.

3.

4.

5.

6.

7.

8.

9.

RESOURCES

If you would like further fun and information about construction vehicles,
check out these books and websites.

BOOKS

Construction Zone series by JoAnn Early Macken
A series geared for beginning readers, but in a picture book format, these have large, clear words with enticing photographs that support the text. Titles include *Construction Tools*, *Construction Crews*, *Building a Skyscraper*, *Building a Road*, *Digging Tunnels*, and *Demolition*.

Heavy Equipment Up Close by Andra Serlin Abramson
Amazing photography and giant pull-out pages make for a fascinating look at construction vehicles and other heavy equipment. This book shows up-close, actual size parts of dump trucks, bucket wheel excavators, super dozers, cranes, and much more. It is a book children will want to look at again and again.

DK Machines at Work series
Written and edited by different authors, this series includes *Truck*, *Digger*, *Crane*, and *Tractor*. Each volume has its own focus. For instance, *Tractor* deals with farm machinery while *Digger* places you at a construction site. All include fabulous photography and interesting facts.

Construction Alphabet Book by Jerry Pallotta
Heavy equipment from A (aerial lift) to Z (zipper) with brief information about each vehicle. Other equipment portrayed include the backhoe, dump truck, jackhammer, borer, loader, crusher, and vactor. Rob Bolster's handsome illustrations will appeal to children.

Mega Trucks by Deborah Murrell and Christiane Gunzi
An oversized format and easy-to-read text make this book very accessible to children. Large, quality photographs are placed throughout the book and interactive questions encourage comprehension in young readers.

The Big Dig: Reshaping an American City by Peter Vanderwarker

A children's guide to the largest public construction project in United States history. It clearly explains how Boston decided to solve their massive traffic problems by creating tunnels under their city and waterways. This plan took years to complete and cost millions and millions of dollars.

WEBSITES

Building Big

www.pbs.org/wgbh/buildingbig

Allows you to explore large structures, such as bridges, dams, skyscrapers, domes, and tunnels, and what it takes to build them. Interactive labs give you a real idea of exactly what is involved in their construction. Additional information is available through interviews with engineers and the Wonders of the World Databank. Based on a PBS special program.

Kikki's Workshop: The Great Picture Book of Construction Equipment

www.kenkenkikki.jp/zukan

This site, sponsored by Komatsu Ltd. of Japan, has pictures and videos of all types of construction vehicles, including dump trucks, bulldozers, loaders, scrapers, rollers, and cranes.

How Stuff Works

www.howstuffworks.com

A website that explains and demonstrates how ANYTHING works. Type the name of a construction vehicle into the search area, and then choose the explanations (words), images (pictures), or videos (to see them in action!) tab.

DLTK's Crafts for Kids: Construction Activities

www.dltk-kids.com/crafts/transportation/construction

This site includes birthday party ideas, coloring pages, snacks, puzzles, and crafts all on a construction work theme. Make a dump truck out of an egg carton or a construction worker from a toilet paper roll. Geared for the younger child.

PUZZLE SOLUTIONS

INTRODUCTION

page 7 • Get Ready for Fun!

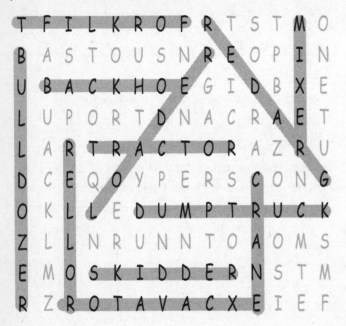

CHAPTER 1

page 10 • Four and More

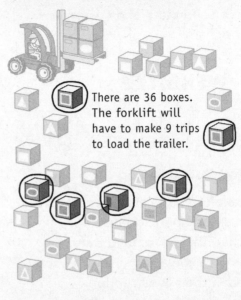

There are 36 boxes. The forklift will have to make 9 trips to load the trailer.

page 11 • Tight Spaces

Just so you know: A multi-terrain loader is a skid steer loader with treads (like a tank) instead of wheels.

page 12 • Floating Cranes

1. B A N A N
2. A R M
3. G U R O
4. E U L

The flat boat that carries a crane is a **BARGE**.

page 13 • Up and Down

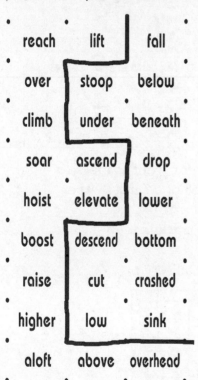

reach	lift	fall
over	stoop	below
climb	under	beneath
soar	ascend	drop
hoist	elevate	lower
boost	descend	bottom
raise	cut	crashed
higher	low	sink
aloft	above	overhead

page 13 • Going Up

A

AN

CAN

CANE

CRANE

page 14 • All in the Name

The bird has a long thin neck and so does the machine. They both use their long neck to pick things up!

page 15 • Junk Pile

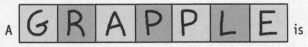

A **GRAPPLE** is a grabbing tool used by cranes to pick up heavy things.

page 16 • Just Joking

None. It was not raining!

page 17 • Egg Drop

THE CRANE DROPPED THE EGG FIFTY-ONE FEET, SO IT DID NOT BREAK FOR THE FIRST FIFTY FEET!

page 18 • Load 'em Up

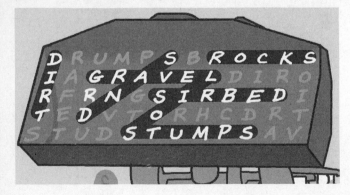

page 18 • Very Versatile

1. RAKE
2. BROOM
3. FORK

page 19 • Way to Move

Some front loaders get around by using

WHEELS

Other front loaders use

TRACKS

It is more popular for front loaders to have wheels instead of tracks. By the way, a front loader that has tracks is usually called a "track loader."

page 20 • Window Delivery

page 22 • Different Dumpers

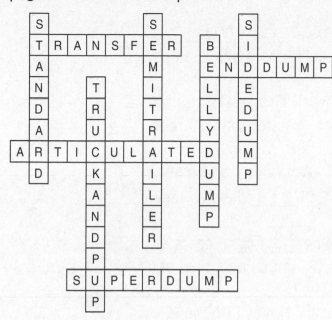

page 23 • Noisy Name

page 24 • Fill 'er Up

JUST 1. AFTER THAT, IT IS NOT EMPTY!

page 25 • Tons of Trash

The following 16 items have been dumped: TICKET, TROPHY, TEDDY BEAR, TOOTHBRUSH, TOOTH, TOP, TIE, TABLE, THIMBLE, TULIP, TUBA, TRAIN, TENT, TOAST, TEAPOT, TEABAG.

page 26 • Safe Travels

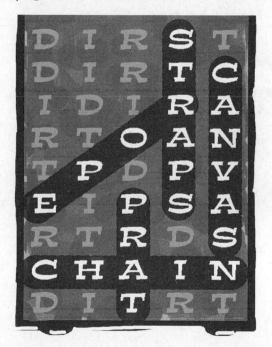

page 26 • Cubic What?

A cubic yard is

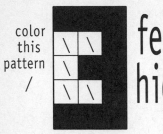

color this pattern /

feet high

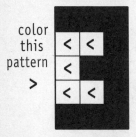

color this pattern >

feet long

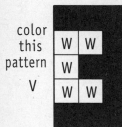

color this pattern v

feet wide

page 27 • Giant Jobs

Driver __cliMbs__ a ladder to reach the cab. | M |

Truck __heIght__ can be greater than 23 feet. | I |

Works day and night, __seveN__ days a week. | N |

One __tIre__ costs as much as a new car. | I |

Moves large loads, __iNcluding__ coal. | N |

Uses six __Gallons__ of fuel to travel one mile. | G |

page 28 • Fast Funny

Oh, I see you are empty!

page 28 • So Big!

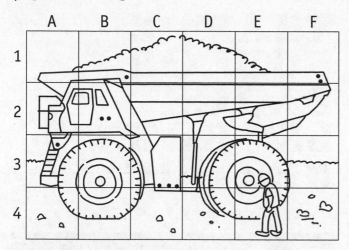

page 30 • Green Tires?

page 30 • Funny Flats

When there is a fork in the road!

page 31 • Twisted Skidders

Skidder #2 is pulling the most shapes (six). Skidders #1 and #3 are only pulling five shapes each. The triangle shape is the only shape that shows up one time.

page 34 • Splash!

The logs get wet!

1. Baby cat — KITTEN
2. Run after — CHASE
3. Sliding snow toy — SLED
4. Under a carpet — FLOOR
5. Jump on one foot — HOP
6. Wine fruit — GRAPE
7. Student's table — DESK
8. Not bad — GOOD
9. Writing tool with ink — PEN
10. Tall rubber shoe — BOOT
11. Spider's trap — WEB
12. Place for a tie — NECK
13. Spinning toy — TOP

page 35 • Very Visible

KYRAEP
BLEB
LEDAS
KGBOZA
JLWESR

page 35 • Push Me, Pull You

page 36 • Big and Small

GIANT SNOWPLOWS CLEAR
AIRPORT RUNWAYS
TINY SNOWPLOWS CLEAR
CITY SIDEWALKS

Fun Fact: The snowplow at the Hancock International Airport in Syracuse, New York might just be the biggest snowplow in the world. The plow's blade is 32 feet long, and 3 inches thick. The 48-inch-tall piece of steel can clear 8,500 cubic yards of snow in one hour!

page 36 • Storm Cleanup

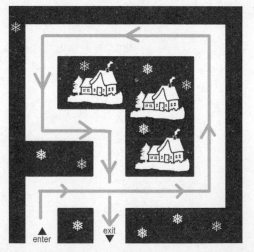

4. R, 2nd L, L, L, L, R

CHAPTER 3

page 37 • What's the Difference?

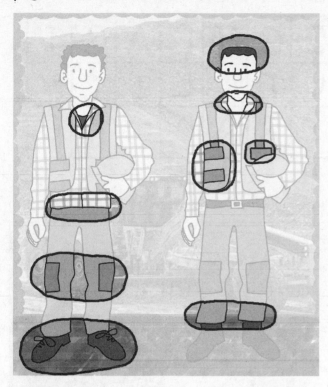

page 38 • Dynamic Duo

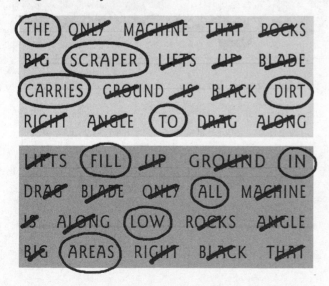

page 39 • World Wide

The largest maker of heavy equipment in the world is:

CATERPILLAR

page 40 • Funny Farmer

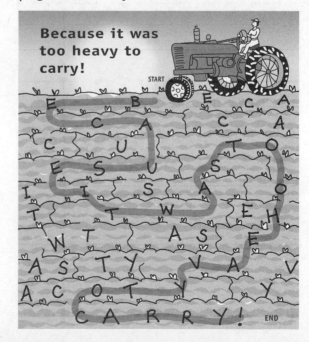

Because it was too heavy to carry!

CHAPTER 3

page 41 • Tractor Treads

THE DEEP TREADS MAKE IT ALMOST IMPOSSIBLE FOR THE TRACTOR TO GET BOGGED DOWN IN THE MUD.

page 41 • Backwards Backfill

END			
SIDE	ROAD	RIGHT	UP
CAR	RAIL	HAND	STICK
SEAT	WAY	STEP	YARD
BELT	DOWN	SIDE	BACK
			START

page 42 • Horse Power

1 HORSEPOWER IS THE ABILITY TO LIFT 33,000 POUNDS ONE FOOT IN ONE MINUTE.

Fun Fact: One average horse actually produces <u>less</u> than one horsepower!

page 43 • Cut Up

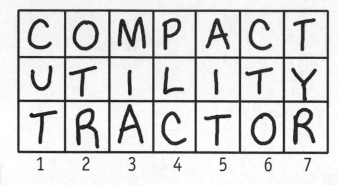

C	O	M	P	A	C	T
U	T	I	L	I	T	Y
T	R	A	C	T	O	R
1	2	3	4	5	6	7

page 43 • Tiny Puzzle

Awww, aren't you CUT<u>E</u>!

page 44 • Wacky Tracks

page 46 • Amazing Inventor

THE DEAN OF EARTHMOVING

page 47 • What Is It?

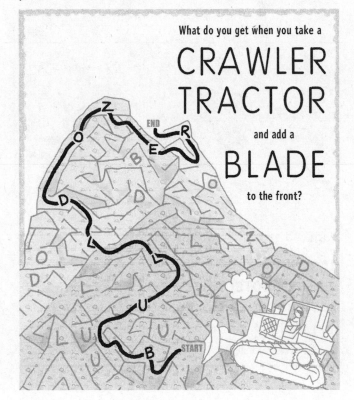

What do you get when you take a

CRAWLER TRACTOR

and add a

BLADE

to the front?

page 48 • Eyes Everywhere Story

Sam was HIRED to operate the hydraulic excavator. He ARRIVED early and CLIMBED into the cab. Sitting BEHIND the controls, Sam used PRECISE movements to safely GUIDE the MIGHTY excavator toward the HILLSIDE. He did not COLLIDE with anything, which is very good! The SUNSHINE was so warm, that Sam began to PERSPIRE. He felt GRIMY, but there was a lot more digging to do. In fact, he ended up working OVERTIME!

page 49 • Eyes Everywhere Search

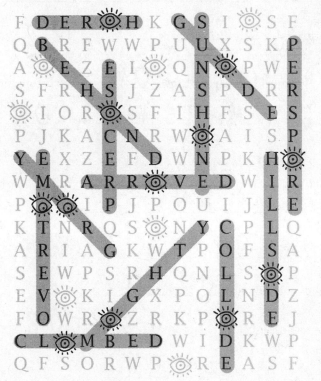

page 50 • Half or Whole?

A. Squirrel food
$\underset{1}{N}\ \underset{7}{U}\ \underset{11}{T}$

B. To postpone
$\underset{12}{D}\ \underset{4}{E}\ \underset{22}{L}\ \underset{19}{A}\ \underset{5}{Y}$

C. On an angel's head
$\underset{15}{H}\ \underset{9}{A}\ \underset{17}{L}\ \underset{2}{O}$

D. Clouds on the ground
$\underset{18}{F}\ \underset{6}{O}\ \underset{14}{G}$

E. Number before two
$\underset{21}{O}\ \underset{3}{N}\ \underset{23}{E}$

F. Linked circles of metal
$\underset{8}{C}\ \underset{20}{H}\ \underset{16}{A}\ \underset{13}{I}\ \underset{10}{N}$

1A	2C	3E	4B		5B	6D	7A
N	O	N	E	.	Y	O	U
8F	**9C**	**10F**		**11A**	**12B**	**13F**	**14D**
C	A	N	'	T	D	I	G
15C	**16F**	**17C**	**18D**	**19B**	**20F**	**21E**	**22B**	**23E**
H	A	L	F	A	H	O	L	E	!

page 51 • Silly Bulldozers

Primary color = **YELLOW**

Campfire treat = **MARSHMALLOW**

Yell loudly = **HOLLER**

A sickness = **ILLNESS**

Pre-butterfly = **CATERPILLAR**

To walk behind = **FOLLOW**

Crocodile cousin = **ALLIGATOR**

Found at the beach = **SHELL**

page 52 • What X-actly Are You?

This machine is an E X C A V A T O R .

page 52 • That's X-citing!

There are 18 Xs hiding in this picture.

page 53 • Head Protection

1. **VISOR**
2. **EAR PROTECTORS**
3. **MIRROR**
4. **LIGHT**
5. **CHIN STRAP**

page 54 • Time to Go

 The circle shape appears only five times. This means that workers must replace their hard hats every five years!

Fun Fact: The first construction site that required all employees to wear hard hats was the Golden Gate Bridge in San Francisco, CA in the 1930s.

page 55 • Opposites

not front → garden tool to remove weeds →

A BACK HOE DIGS

not push →

BY PULL ING DIRT

not front → BACK WARDS. A

soil ↗

raises up →

BULL DOZE R LIFTS DIRT

male cow — sleep lightly — not pull — not backward

BY PUSH ING IT FORWARD.

page 56 • Work Days

PULL ON SUNDAY, PLOW ON MONDAY.

CHAPTER 5

page 58 • Rat-a-tat-tat

WORKERS CHIP OUT THE HARD CEMENT WITH JACKHAMMERS OR SOMETIMES DYNAMITE

page 58 • Ready Made

1. CEMENT
2. WATER
3. GRAVEL
4. SAND

Most people think "cement" and "concrete" are the same thing. Actually, cement is one of the ingredients that make concrete! So, there is no such thing as a "cement mixer." Its proper name is "concrete mixer"!

page 59 • Back End

A concrete mixer that unloads from the back is called a "BUTT DUMPER."

page 59 • Mix It Up

page 60 • Hard Stuff

S L U M P

page 61 • Step by Step

page 62 • Silly Sentences

Harry Heaved His Heavy Hydraulic Hammer.

Ronald Recklessly Rolled Right.

Jerry's Jackhammer Just Jumped.

Carl's Concrete Cracked Crookedly.

Mike's Mixer Made Marvelous Mud.

page 62 • Word Merge

Two colors = **ORANGE & YELLOW**

Two animals = **ELEPHANT & MONKEY**

Two numbers = **FOURTEEN & ELEVEN**

Two states = **WISCONSIN & IDAHO**

Two fruits = **CHERRIES & APPLES**

Two flowers = **DAFFODIL & CARNATION**

page 63 • Good Vibrations

Possible Answers: AN, ANT, AS, AT, BAN, BARN, BARON, BAT, BIN, BIT, BOAR, BORN, BRA, BRAIN, BRAN, BRAT, IN, INTO, IONS, IRON, IS, IT, NIT, NO, OAR, ON, ONTO, OR, ORB, ORBIT, RAIN, RAN, RAT, RATION, RIB, ROBIN, SAT, SAVIOR, SIN, SIT, SNOB, SO, SOAR, SOB, SON, STRAIN, TAN, TIS, TON, TORN, TRAIN, TRIVIA, VAIN, VAN, VAST, VAT, VISIT, VISOR, VISTA, VISITOR.
Answers of five letters or more are highlighted.

page 63 • Dangerous Noise

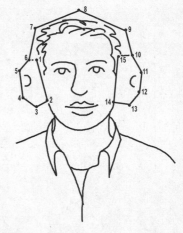

THEY WEAR SAFETY EARMUFFS

Special safety earmuffs block sound and protect the inner ear from damage.

page 64 • Pound the Ground

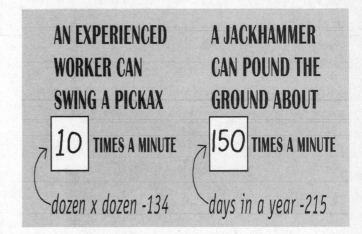

AN EXPERIENCED WORKER CAN SWING A PICKAX

10 TIMES A MINUTE

dozen x dozen -134

A JACKHAMMER CAN POUND THE GROUND ABOUT

150 TIMES A MINUTE

days in a year -215

page 64 • J Is for Jackhammer

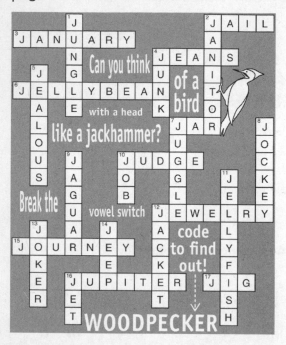

page 67 • Crazy Maze

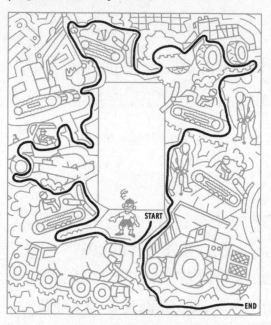

page 66 • Away It Goes

page 68 • Safety First

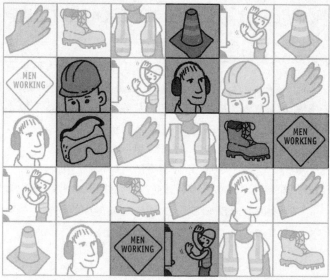

The safety goggles appear only once.

page 70 • Shake, Rattle . . .

To break the code, you must look at it in a mirror! It reads:

HEAVY WEIGHTS INSIDE THE ROLLING DRUM SLAM DOWN CAUSING POWERFUL VIBRATIONS THAT PACK DIRT DOWN TIGHT.

page 70 • . . . and Roll

Sign up to join a club =
E N R O L L

Fairy tale creature under a bridge =
T R O L L

Streetcar that runs on tracks =
T R O L L E Y

A slow walk =
S T R O L L

page 71 • What If . . .

page 72 • Dumb Cluck

page 73 • Squash It Flat

Today the landfill compactor has squashed a trumpet, pair of scissors, bike, mug, fork, tennis racket, umbrella, rocking chair, coat hanger, and floor lamp.

page 74 • Hot Worker, Cool Worker

page 75 • Big Breaker

page 76 • Caution Ahead!

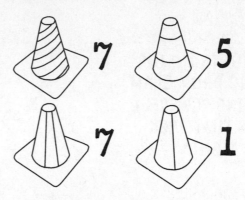

page 78 • Pick a Pile

1. WOOD
2. STEEL
3. CONCRETE

page 79 • Going Down

Pile 1: Choose even numbers			Pile 2: Choose numbers divisible by 3		
68	70	72	99	90	88
56	67	69	98	96	97
51	50	49	95	94	90
52	54	44	92	91	87
47	42	46	86	75	74
38	43	45	88	70	69
35	32	31	71	60	55
34	30	33	58	54	61
27	25	26	56	53	51
21	28	22	43	44	42
24	20	23	31	28	30
19	15	16	19	20	21

page 80 • BOOM! BOOM! BOOM! BOOM!

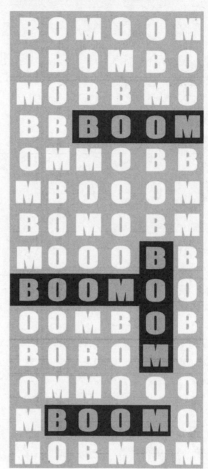

page 80 • Shake It Down

THEY ARE LESS NOISY

Fun Fact: This type of hammer can also shake a pile loose so it can be removed!

CHAPTER 7

page 82 • Very Boring

page 83 • High and Low

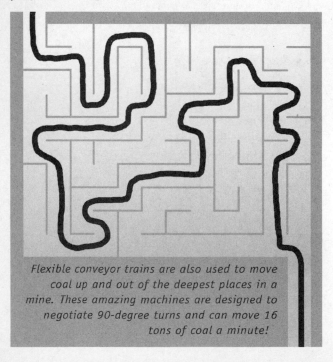

Flexible conveyor trains are also used to move coal up and out of the deepest places in a mine. These amazing machines are designed to negotiate 90-degree turns and can move 16 tons of coal a minute!

page 84 • Make a Ditch

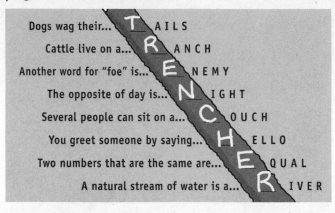

Dogs wag their... **T** AILS

Cattle live on a... **R** ANCH

Another word for "foe" is... **E** NEMY

The opposite of day is... **N** IGHT

Several people can sit on a... **C** OUCH

You greet someone by saying... **H** ELLO

Two numbers that are the same are... **E** QUAL

A natural stream of water is a... **R** IVER

page 85 • Ahhh! Grrr!

The first word is AUGER. Another name for an auger is a DRILL.

page 85 • Ha Ha

What grows larger the more you take away? A HOLE!

page 86 • Street Scramble

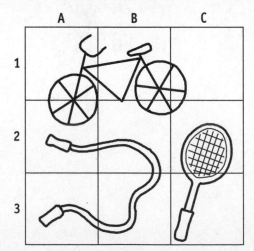

page 87 • Hurry Harvester

It takes less than thirty seconds.

page 88 • Cut & Drill

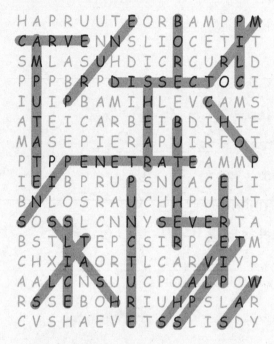

page 89 • Zappy Zipper

EACH **ACHE**
dull pain

BELOW **ELBOW**
arm joint

BLOW **BOWL**
cereal holder

ODOR **DOOR**
house exit

LEAF **FLEA**
dog biter

TONES **STONE**
rock

page 89 • Road Repair

RECYCLING

page 90 • Stumped

It will take 270 minutes (4.5 hours) to grind all the stumps in the field.

page 91 • What a Wall!

Fun Fact: Started in 1991, the Big Dig is the largest public construction project in United States history!

page 92 • Holey Schmoley!

EXPLOSIVES

page 94 • Useful Utilities

G A S

E L E C T R I C

T E L E P H O N E

C A B L E

W A T E R

page 95 • Picky, Picky

Score between poles 1 and 2: 34

Score between poles 2 and 3: 43

Score between poles 3 and 4: 29

page 96 • Help Is on the Way

What did the ballerina do when she hurt her foot?

1 S	2 H	3 E		4 C	5 A	6 L	7 L	8 E	9 D
			10 T	11 H	12 E				
13 T	14 O	15 E		16 T	17 R	18 U	19 C	20 K	!

A. Money to cross a bridge
T O L L
10 14 7 6

B. Hot road covering
T A R
16 5 17

C. Side of your face
C H E E K
19 2 12 8 20

D. Small storage building
S H E D
1 11 3 9

E. How a baby looks
C U T E
4 18 13 15

page 97 • Fast Fixers

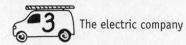 The electric company

 The gas company

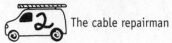 The cable repairman

page 97 • Gas Leak

Long stories = S A G A S

Sudden breath = G A S P

A deep cut = G A S H

Roman garments = T O G A S

White whales = B E L U G A S

page 98 • Patching Potholes

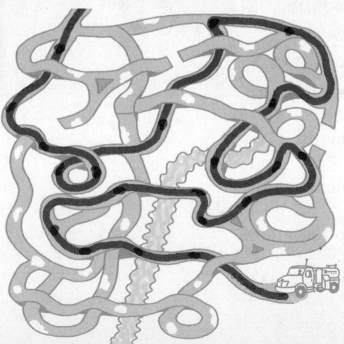

CHAPTER 8

page 99 • Thanks, Cookie

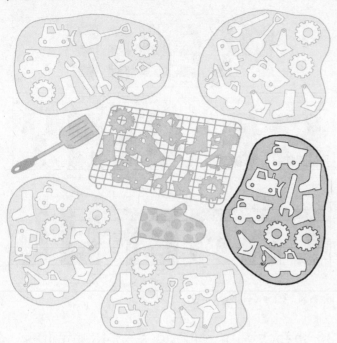

page 102 • Flooding Foolery

Teddy into an autumn fruit
B E A R to P E A R

Shellfish into a baby sheep
C L A M to L A M B

Wooden box into a dish
C R A T E to P L A T E

Small stream into seven days
C R E E K to W E E K

Dried fruit into a small branch
F I G to T W I G

Sleeveless shirt into a visitor
V E S T to G U E S T

page 103 • Drain Debris

DITCH	CATCH	REACH	DIRT
LEAKS	DEBRIS	HASTE	GALE
FLOOD	PIT	BASIN	WET
DEEP	CLEAN	HURRICANE	TASTE
BASTE	LEAVES	DRIPS	FLOAT

page 104 • What Am I?

STREET SWEEPER

CHAPTER 9

page 106 • Something to Nothing

page 107 • All Clear

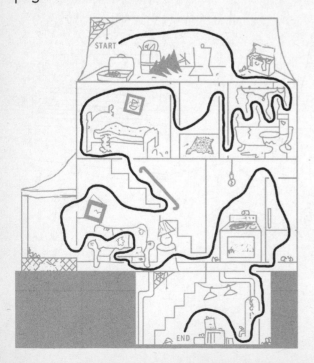

page 108 • Spectators at the Site

page 110 • Get a Grip

36 shapes with four sides = 540 minutes
6 shapes with three sides = 180 minutes
4 irregular shapes = 240 minutes

Total minutes = 960
Divide by 60 = 16 hours

CHAPTER 9

page 111 • DY-NO-MITE!

TO DESTROY A HIGHRISE BUILDING

page 111 • What a Wreck!

page 112 • Helping Hands

4 Clearing Rake
2 Concrete Pulverizer
1 Grapple
3 Metal Shears

page 113 • Crazy Close-Ups

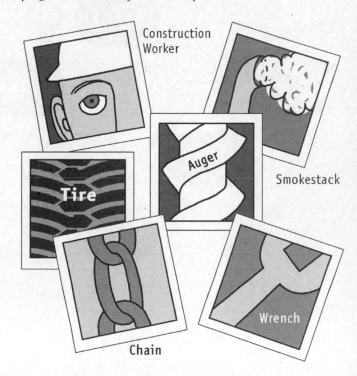

Construction Worker

Smokestack

Auger

Tire

Chain

Wrench

page 114 • Super Suction

AFTER A FLOOD OR HURRICANE

page 115 • Danger Dude

page 117 • Look Again!

1. Just Joking

2. Twisted Skidders

3. Splash!

4. That's X-citing!

5. Away It Goes

6. Shake It Down

7. AHHH! GRRR!

8. Picky, Picky

9. Super Suction